The English Market Town

**This book is to be returned on or before
the last date stamped below.**

ce

LIBREX

The English Market Town

A SOCIAL AND ECONOMIC HISTORY 1750-1914

JONATHAN BROWN

The Crowood Press

First published in 1986 by
THE CROWOOD PRESS
Crowood House, Ramsbury,
Marlborough, Wiltshire SN8 2HE

British Library Cataloguing in Publication Data

Brown, Jonathan
The English market town:
a social and economic history 1750-1914
1.   Market towns – England – History
I.   Title
307.7′63′0942   HT 133

Picture Credits

Carlisle Museum and Art Gallery: *page 31*
Dorchester County Museum: *pages 109, 131*
Elmbridge Borough Council, Weybridge Museum: *page 81*
Farnham Museum: *page 122 (bottom)*
Godalming Museum: *pages 55, 57*
Mrs S. Hopson: *pages 143, 149, 169*
Chris Howell: *page 61*
Mrs Iris Moon: *page 133*
North Hertfordshire District Council, Hitchin Museum:
pages 23, 83, 115, 124, 135
Northamptonshire County Record Office: *pages 17, 35*
Topham Picture Library: *page 51*
University of Reading Institute of Agricultural History &
Museum of English Rural Life: *pages 9, 13, 14, 20, 29, 34, 37,
43, 45, 47, 49, 54, 59, 66, 67, 73, 85, 89, 91, 93, 95, 97, 99,
103, 105, 107, 108, 122 (top), 125, 128, 130, 139, 147, 150,
155, 159, 161, 165*
Reading Museum and Art Gallery: front jacket

The diagram on page 119 was drawn by Vanetta Joffe

Typeset by Alacrity Phototypesetters, Weston-super-Mare
Printed in Great Britain

Contents

Preface

The market town is a traditional and familiar part of the English scene; so much so that it tends to be taken for granted. Yet these towns have seen many vicissitudes during the centuries, some of which have affected them more than others. One of the greatest challenges faced by the market town was the period when farming was declining in importance in the English economy, and industry was rapidly taking its place. These changes struck at the roots of the market town's existence, and it is with the effect of these pressures that this book is concerned. It follows, then, that this is primarily a social and economic history.

In a volume this size it is impossible to give detailed coverage of all the hundreds of market towns in the country. It has been necessary to be selective, using the experiences of some towns to demonstrate the changes affecting most, if not all. To a considerable extent the selection has been determined by the three or four parts of the country in which my own research has been concentrated. These alone, however, would have been insufficient and a great debt is owed to the dozens of authors, past and present, who have written about the regions, counties and individual towns of this country. In particular, I am grateful to the amateur historians, often working under the auspices of the Workers' Educational Association, who painstakingly analyse local records, such as the census returns. Books such as this would be the poorer without their work. This book, however, has been written without detailed references; instead, every published source used directly is included in the bibliography.

I am indebted to many for their help both during the writing and with the compilation of illustrations. I am particularly grateful to Sadie Ward at Reading University's Institute of Agricultural History for reading and suggesting improvements to the manuscript. My thanks also to John Dennis at The Crowood Press who has been encouraging and patient and to Nan Ridehalgh for compiling the index. Finally, I am grateful to my parents who helped with checking references and typing the text.

Introduction

'There are few things which give one such a feeling of the prosperity of the country, as seeing the country people pour into a large town on market day. There they come, streaming along all the roads that lead to it from the wide country round. The footpaths are filled with a hardy and homely succession of pedestrians, men and women, with their baskets on their arms, containing their butter, eggs, apples, mushrooms, walnuts, nuts, elderberries, blackberries, bundles of herbs, young pigeons, fowls, or whatever happens to be in season ... the carriage road is equally alive with people riding or driving along; farmers and country gentlemen, country clergymen, parish overseers, and various other personages, drawn to the market town by some real or imagined business, are rattling forward on horseback, or in carriages of various kinds ... There are carriers' wagons, and covered carts without end, many of them shewing from their open fronts whole troops of women snugly seated ...'

Thus wrote William Howitt in the 1830s, half-way through the period covered by this book, describing something of the essence of market town life, which had been as true in 1750 and was still true, though to a lesser extent, in 1914. The market town served the needs of the countryside. Through it was channelled most of the buying and selling of the produce of the farms, and it also served the domestic needs of the villagers.

The markets, held regularly once or twice a week, and the fairs, which took place at set times in the year, were central to the market town's activities. Market-day was the big day for the townspeople as much as for the villagers. This was the day when the shopkeepers did a roaring trade, the inns were busy and the solicitors and bankers received their farming clients. At the end of the day all the visitors went back to the villages, leaving the town in relative peace until the next market-day came round. But the townsmen did not just sit back and wait for the villagers to come in. The relationship between the town and its countryside was much more intimate. 'No matter what a man's trade or profession', wrote George Sturt of mid-nineteenth century Farnham, 'linen-draper, or saddler, or baker, or lawyer, or banker, he found it worth while to watch the harvests, and to know a great deal about cattle and sheep, and more than a great deal about hops'. Some of the tradesmen were, in fact, growing wealthy as hop-planters; and one and all identified themselves with the outdoor industries of the neighbourhood. Indeed, identification with the outdoor industries was more than nominal. Labourers from the town would go out and take casual work in the fields at peak times. There were farmers and their labourers living in the towns into the mid-nineteenth century. Grantham, no mean town by 1851 with a population of 10,781, had fifteen farmers giving central addresses in the directory for 1856. Melbourne in Derbyshire had 189 agricultural labourers living in the town according to the 1851 census.

The market town's fortunes, therefore, were closely bound up with those of agriculture. For most of the period covered by this book agricultural progress can be said to have benefited the country town. For this was the time of the agricultural revolution, when ancient open fields were being enclosed; farmers were increasing the produce of their land by adopting new rotations, by sowing new crops such as clover and turnips, and by using more fertilisers and new farm implements; they produced more animal products by keeping improved breeds and by using concentrated feedstuffs. All of this meant that the output of farming was increasing, and most of the greater volume of produce was sold through the country markets. In turn this brought business to the tradesmen of the town: the corn dealers, millers, dealers in feeds and fertilisers, implement makers and sellers, leather workers and the host of other merchants and trades-men closely involved with agriculture. Prosperous agriculture increased the demands on the town's shopkeepers, who gained more custom from farmers, labourers and the gentry who, with rising rent rolls, could increase their patronage of the more genteel shops. The gentry would also give generous support to the improvement of the town and to local charities.

But agricultural progress was not an unending upward movement. There were down periods, and on those occasions the town suffered just as much as the country. The inhabitants of Colchester petitioned Parliament in 1820 to do something to restore agriculture's fortunes which had been depressed since 1816 because 'your petitioners are

The country market – an engraving from Jeffreys Taylor's book
The Farm, published in 1832.

entirely dependent upon agriculture for support'. When a parliamentary inquiry into the plight of farming was held the next year, tradesmen from Colchester gave evidence of wheelwrights, blacksmiths and others being in difficulties because farmers were unable to pay their bills. The deepest depression descended upon farming in the last quarter of the nineteenth century. Arable farming suffered especially as cheap imported grain undermined the cereal grower's business. Tradesmen in the market towns felt the impact of farming's problems. In particular, those in the corn-growing south and east of England were hit. The industries of Newark-upon-Trent were in difficulties, and 'without a revival of agriculture the depression in the home market must continue and probably increase'. The largest employers at Banbury, the agricultural engineers Samuelsons, had their men on short time in 1880. The small tradesmen similarly suffered, such as the ironmonger in Peterborough who blamed his bankruptcy in 1890 on the agricultural depression, which meant that fewer people came into town for the Saturday market.

The agricultural revolution was not the only major influence on the prosperity of the market towns. Of even greater importance, perhaps, was the growth of modern industry. The industrial revolution affected country towns in several ways. Firstly, the new towns housing the industrial workers offered ready markets for agricultural produce and, therefore, brought trade into the country markets. In return, industry could offer an improved standard of living to the people of the market towns through the supply of cheap, mass-produced food products and domestic goods. But in bringing the advantages of new factory-made goods, the industrial revolution undermined the traditional economy of the market town. Old crafts, trades and industries went into decline, unable to compete with the factories of the North and Midlands, either in price or in the fashionable range of designs on offer. One of the most striking examples of this change was the virtual disappearance of the textile industries of southern England, which had been founded upon the local supply of wool. The new factories of the eighteenth and nineteenth centuries went to the northern coalfields, leaving many a town in the south stripped of its former prosperity. In the early eighteenth century Harlow had a large corn market and was a busy centre of the woollen trade. A hundred years later,

'the factories ... are closed; the manufacture departed; the market decayed; the wool fair, which long survived, was at last discontinued; the rail came and robbed the town of its through traffic, and it is now a clean little country town ... and little to distinguish it from an ordinary Essex village, save that it is the capital of the Hundred, and has a neat little police station ...'

While towns in the south were being forced back to a closer dependence on the surrounding farmland through the loss of the manufacturing part of their economy, there were others in the North that were being transformed into predominantly industrial towns. In the Yorkshire woollen district the long-established cloth-making and merchanting trades, which were already the mainstay of towns such as Halifax in the early eighteenth century, achieved dominance as business moved from workshops to factories. The new steam-powered cotton mills in Lancashire began to congregate around established towns, such as Bury and Chorley. Even such a small place as Wigton in Cumberland, away from the mainstream of industrialisation, gained a new prosperity from factories weaving woollen and linen cloth which were set up here in the second half of the eighteenth century.

The iron and engineering industries were another major force changing the economic shape of old market towns. Towns in the rapidly industrialising areas of the North and Midlands again were usually those affected first and most deeply. Darlington was one of these, where the combined effects of the railway and the opening of the Cleveland iron ore field were to reduce the old rural marketing and servicing trades to a small fragment of the town's life. During the second half of the nineteenth century these and other industries were growing in importance in some of the market towns of southern England. By 1914 Peterborough derived much of its prosperity from brickworks and general engineering, Colchester was noted for its engineering factories and Old Swindon was dwarfed by the railway works of New Swindon. Reading had grown on the strength of its brickyards, brewery and biscuit factory, all of which had outgrown their country town origins to become major suppliers to the whole of southern England. In the mid-nineteenth century Reading was one of the towns of England whose population was growing most rapidly, and the expansion of its industries was such that by 1900 it was said of the town that it was 'formerly dependent on the country around for its trade'.

It is at this point that one might ask whether Reading could still be called a market town or whether it had joined the ranks of what the 1851 census called towns of 'adventitious character', where existence was dependent mainly on manufacturing, mining, leisure and other activities. 'Towns of this class', continued the same report on the census, 'are, considered only in their local relations, naturally towns of an inferior order; and even in advanced periods of British history several of them were villages or small market towns'. Defining a market town is not a straightforward task. The pace of change differed widely between regions of the country, so that the question just asked of Reading in 1890 might equally have been asked of Darlington fifty years previously, of Bury a few years before that, or of Halifax even in the early eighteenth century when Daniel Defoe regarded it as more of a manufacturing than a market town. The size of a town is no sure guide. The term market town could embrace some of the great county and provincial centres, such as Northampton and Norwich, and equally some really small places like Harrold and Shefford in Bedfordshire, which in the late eighteenth century contained no more than 700 and 400 people respectively. There was no shortage of villages larger than these two towns: Eaton Socon, still in Bedfordshire, had more than 1,000 inhabitants as early as 1671.

What marked off the Sheffords from the Eaton Socons was that the towns contained a greater range of the more specialised industries and services. This in turn was often a matter of status and history. Before the industrial revolution came to create new manufacturing centres, nearly all the towns of England had grown up from early settlements or had been founded as towns. Most of these foundations had been in the Middle Ages. The kings and great landowners who promoted them set out to attract the tradesmen, craftsmen, merchants and manufacturers who would provide the rents the patrons were looking for and whose business could not usually be supported by a village. The most important mark of urban status bestowed by the founders was the grant of the right to hold a market, since the towns were there to promote the development of trade. The privilege of holding markets and fairs was granted by royal charter, although there were quite a few private, and therefore in strict terms illegal, markets which were successfully developed. On this basis then, definition becomes simple: if a place has a market, it is a town. But that is no help in dealing with the towns which had outgrown their country origins by the eighteenth and nineteenth centuries. Manchester, Leeds and Liverpool all had markets, but they will not feature largely in these pages.

At the other end of the scale, possession of a market can be useful in making the distinction between a small town and a large village. Even then, the possession of market rights was no guarantee of a town's success. More towns were founded in medieval times than the agriculture and commerce of the nation could support. Towns slipped back to become villages, though retaining perhaps a few signs of their urban origins, such as a larger number of craftsmen amongst the population than would be found in most villages. Some market

A hop fair at Reading in 1859. This new venture was an attempt to broaden the commerce of the town through the opportunities brought by the railway. It was however short-lived.

towns were failures almost from their foundation. New Eagle, for example, was unhappily sited half-way between Lincoln and Newark in a district too desolate for anyone to want to live there. Its foundation shortly before the Black Death probably did not further the town's success. The commonest cause for a town's failure was competition from a larger neighbour. Thatcham, four miles down an easy road from Newbury in Berkshire, could never hope to attract trade from the established town, and its urban existence barely survived the end of the Middle Ages. As transport improved, so the distance goods and people could easily travel to market increased, thus some towns grew at the expense of others. This was a common strand running through all centuries, but after 1750 the rate at which communications improved and the effect of this on small towns was greater.

A sheep fair at East Ilsley just before the First World War.

A simple counting of the numbers of markets can show the effect of these changes during this period. According to *Magnae Britanniae Notitia* published in 1748, there were 681 market towns in England. Owen's *Book of Fairs* for 1792 lists some 550 places where regular markets were held; and the reports of the Royal Commission on Market Rights and Tolls in the 1880s number only about 380 market towns. These figures can serve only as a rough guide however, for there were inaccuracies in the lists arising mainly from the difficulty of determining whether the smaller places with barely functioning markets could still count as towns. There were a few small, but thriving, places which did not fit easily into any classification. East Ilsley, in Berkshire, held sheep markets (or fairs, the terms being used loosely here) every fortnight for most of the year. They were impressive, attracting several thousand sheep for sale most weeks, and had a far-ranging reputation. These fairs established Ilsley's claim for inclusion as one of Berkshire's market towns, yet in almost every other respect it was no more than a large village of 700 people in the mid-nineteenth century.

From this discussion it is clear that finding a neat definition for the market town between 1750 and 1914 is really impossible. Nor does that failure matter very much, because it is with the processes of growth and decline that this book is primarily concerned. Harlow, with its neat police station a sign of past glory, and Reading, with its biscuits and beer transforming it into a modern manufacturing and commercial town, both have their place in the story. The criterion for inclusion here is the connection between the town and its countryside, and clearly the closeness of that connection was constant neither in place nor time.

=1=
Markets and Fairs

Market-day was the highlight of the week for the country town. There were several different markets busy at the same time, vying for space in the confines of the town centre. The farmers and agricultural merchants had come to town for the corn and cattle markets. Sometimes, mainly in the larger towns, there might be other markets for farm produce, such as hides, wool or cheese. Meanwhile, the farmers' wives, smallholders and allotment holders had come to sell their fruit and vegetables, butter, eggs and poultry in the general retail market. There was something for everybody in this market, from food to clothing, household goods, and farm tools and machinery.

As well as the regular weekly markets, there were fairs held at set times during the year. Some of the busier towns had quite a collection of fairs; Loughborough in the mid-nineteenth century had as many as eight, but for most places, three or four was adequate. Most fairs were held for the sale of livestock, but until railways and the growth of shops gave a more regular supply, there were important retail-cum-wholesale fairs for general household goods, such as pots and pans, wooden bowls and toys. There were other more specialised fairs; towns in the West Country had cheese fairs, and Retford was noted for its fair for hops until the mid-nineteenth century when hop-growing declined in Nottinghamshire.

Not all fairs were held in the market towns. Several took place in villages, often for ancient reasons, such as if the site was on a meeting point at a parish boundary or on an ancient trackway – there were some of these fairs on the cattle droving routes through the Pennines. Other fairs were in villages just outside the town in order to avoid the jurisdiction of borough authorities. Whatever the reason, some of the biggest fairs in the country were held in these villages. Weyhill, near Andover, was one, famous for its sheep fairs; another was Sturbridge fair, just outside Cambridge, where almost anything

A wool fair at Brackley, Northamptonshire, in 1910.

could be bought and sold.

The more ancient fairs had their origins in religious festivities, and visitors might need a reliable almanac to make sure that they knew when the Friday before old Michaelmas was going to fall that year. It was not always necessary to be that exact though, for the fairs might have been like the two at Warrington which each lasted for ten days, 'when considerable transactions take place in the sale and purchase of woollen cloths, horses, horned cattle, sheep, pigs, and pedlery'. Sturbridge outdid most others, running for three weeks in August and September.

The agricultural markets, the retail markets and the shops were to a considerable extent dependent upon each other. In November 1853, the farmers and agricultural traders set up a new corn market at Droitwich in Worcestershire. It did not last a full year. It was suggested at the time that one of the major reasons for its failure was that the farmers' wives preferred Worcester or Bromsgrove, 'where the drapers' shops had a variety of goods for sale'.

CORN MARKETS

Once a week, perhaps twice a week in a few of the larger towns, farmers came to sell their corn to the merchants, millers and maltsters. In the eighteenth century, they might meet to conduct business in the open market-place, under the arches of the market hall, or often in the yards and upper rooms of one or more of the inns around the market-place. These inns may not have been the official places in which to transact business, but they had the considerable advantages of warmth, comfort and hospitality. William Marshall discovered how these trading arrangements worked when he visited North Walsham market in Norfolk in the 1780s:

'Having made my selection of a miller, and finding that he "quartered" at the Bear, I went to his room . . . and shewed him my sample: namely about two handfulls put in a piece of brown paper; which agreeable to the fashion of the country, was gathered up in the hand, and tied with string, in the manner of a pounce bag . . . His room was set around with farmers, who, the conversation being audible, were witnesses to the bargain'.

Like most corn markets, North Walsham's was not open all day. This was an afternoon market, and the miller William Marshall wanted to see apparently did not usually attend until about six o'clock. Others, probably the majority, confined trading to the morning. After the business was over the farmers, together perhaps with some of the merchants, gathered at their favourite inn for the 'market ordinary' dinner where they would settle a few debts and discuss the woes of the farming world.

The market at North Walsham was a sample market. The deal was struck on the basis of a sample bag of grain which the farmer showed the buyer. The bulk of the produce could then be delivered direct from the farm to the merchant's granary. The alternative to this arrangement was the pitched market, which could be found at Warminster, Wiltshire to the end of the nineteenth century. Every Saturday morning, the farmers' wagons came into town bringing all the corn they were offering for sale that day. The wagons were placed in store – the yard or a barn attached to the inns around the market-place. A sample sack was taken out and 'pitched' in the market for the buyers to inspect. There might be room under cover of the old market hall to stand the sacks, but Warminster was not unusual in having no such accommodation. The sacks were given a bedding of straw to keep them off the ground, but they were out in the open whatever the weather. At Wigton in Cumberland, stone setts formed into the letters W, B and O marked the places where the wheat, barley and oats should be pitched.

The relative merits of selling corn by sample or in a pitched market were the subject of debate from time to time. Daniel Defoe was one of those fiercely opposed to sample markets. Pitched markets were more honest, he argued, because the buyer could go and look at the full wagon-load if he wanted, an argument that was repeated down the years. The pitched market was also favoured by those amongst the labouring classes of the town who derived valuable casual employment as corn porters, heaving the sacks from wagon to market. Occasionally a market might change from selling by sample to pitching. This happened at Wantage in the 1840s and was held to be one of the main reasons for a revival of trade here. Devizes and Salisbury had busy pitched markets into the 1860s, and at Yeovil trade was so great that the new market hall needed extending.

The general trend in the later nineteenth century was against the pitched market. For one thing, as Yeovil's experience shows, sacks needed space on the floor while sample bags took up pocket room only. In addition, pitched markets had other drawbacks. Wagons travelled slowly, and took a lot of horse- and manpower. In the early nineteenth century, sending a load of wheat about twenty-five miles from Eastdean to Horsham in Sussex, occupied the farmer, his carter and a boy, and four horses for two days. Wagons going to Reading market from fifteen miles away in Hampshire would set out at midnight to reach the town about six in the morning. When it became possible to make that journey by train in perhaps half an hour the inconvenience of taking up so much time and labour was heightened. Eventually farmers and dealers opted for the convenience of sample bags.

During the mid-nineteenth century, special corn exchanges were built to house the corn market in a number of towns. These buildings offered spacious halls in which the dealers set up their stands, it being commonly felt that such accommodation would be an improvement

19

Newark corn exchange. Opened in 1849, it presents the typical
architectural style of these buildings: a clock tower, statues
of Agriculture and Commerce, and carvings of sheaves of corn
decorating the spandrils of the archways.

upon the open market-place, the inn yards or the space under the old
town hall. There was ample justification for this, as can be seen from
reports such as those in the *Berkshire Mercury* in January 1852 about
heavy rain disrupting the markets in Swindon and Newbury. Stormy
weather was not, however, the most compelling reason for building a
new market hall. There were two other, largely complementary
reasons why this investment was thought worth while. The first was
that the trade in corn was increasing at this time as more grain was
being grown, and it was felt that an expanding market deserved good
accommodation. The second was the belief that a well-equipped
market would attract more buyers and sellers. This was partly a
reflection of the general expansion in the corn trade, but was also an
effect of inter-town rivalry, for once one town had a good corn

exchange, its neighbours and competitors were likely to follow suit for fear of losing trade to it.

Such rivalry no doubt accounts for the rapid succession in which corn exchanges were built. The pioneering towns had exchanges built in the 1820s and 1830s; Stamford's, for example, was built in 1839. But most were built in the period from about 1848 to 1865. Of the nineteen towns of Lincolnshire with corn markets of any size, fifteen acquired modern corn exchanges, and all of these (except for the one at Stamford) were built between 1847 and 1857. This pattern was repeated throughout the corn-growing counties of eastern and southern England. In the west, where corn was not always so important, fewer corn exchanges were built; instead, sample markets found accommodation in other buildings. In Worcestershire, a corn exchange was built at Kidderminster in 1855 and at Tenbury in 1858, but at Upton upon Severn and Bewdley the market met in the town hall.

As well as offering better housing for the corn market, the new exchange could become a valuable addition to the town's public buildings, available for public meetings, concerts, dances and exhibitions. This aspect of the building's functions explains the keenness to have handsome styling, usually in the new vernacular styles, such as the 'Italianate' or the 'Elizabethan', which were coming into vogue at this time. Impressive sums were sometimes spent; the exchange at Newbury, built in 1861–2, was one of the more expensive, costing £6,000; most cost between £2,000 and £3,000. Keeping up with the neighbouring towns again had some influence on the architecture and cost of these buildings. Usually the corn exchange was the work of a private company whose shareholders came from amongst the wealthy of the town.

Occasionally, two rival halls were built. This happened at Grantham in 1852, causing the contributor to the county directory to complain that the rivalry in the corn market: 'gives much dissatisfaction to the farmers and dealers, and it is hoped that the proprietors of the two handsome and commodious buildings will, ere long, so far amalgamate their interests as to have the corn market altogether in one of the halls, each of which will seat 800 people'. Even such generous provision could not always break old habits. Banbury also had two rival corn exchanges, one in Cornhill, the other in Market Place. 'Corn transactions were officially done at the latter', writes one of the town's historians, 'but the real corn market was at the Red Lion'.

A busy corn market could present a crowded scene. Farnham was reputedly the largest market for wheat in the kingdom in the early eighteenth century. It was so vast that, according to a remarkably perspicuous informant of Daniel Defoe's 'he once counted on a market day eleven hundred teams of horse . . . every team of which is supposed to bring what they call a load, that is to say forty bushel of wheat, to market, which is in the whole, four and forty thousand bushel'. A trade of 44,000 bushels at one market was certainly a remarkable volume, though it is possible that the accuracy of the gentleman's tally was not perfect.

In the mid-nineteenth century the official reports on the corn trade at Boston regularly returned figures of over 4,000 quarters for the weekly trade in wheat, and sometimes turnover could reach 9,000 quarters.[1] More corn was being grown by this time, but these figures are little different from those suggested for Farnham more than a hundred years before. In the 1850s, Boston was certainly a contender for the position of the busiest corn market outside London, especially for dealings in wheat. Few other markets, even in the major centres such as Salisbury and Bury St Edmunds, reported trade much more than half that of Boston. When it came to barley however, Boston was easily outclassed, not being in a major barley-growing part of the country.

Farnham, meanwhile, had long since lost its standing in the hierarchy of markets. Even at the time Daniel Defoe was writing in the 1720s, the town's importance in the grain trade was beginning to decline. Wheat which in times past had been brought into Farnham from Sussex and Hampshire, was now being sold through local markets to millers around Chichester and Southampton. This trend continued through the eighteenth century so that by 1800, Farnham's corn market was of modest proportions, and the town's trade was now concentrated on hops. Although more pronounced than most, the decline of Farnham's grain trade was just one of many changes in the pattern of trade.

---

[1] Throughout the period of this book, corn was bought and sold in bushels and quarters. These were measures of volume, and weights varied between the different types of grain, and between different qualities of the same grain. Standard weights for a quarter were 512 lb wheat and 448 lb barley. There were eight bushels to a quarter.

The interior of Hitchin corn exchange. Taken about 1917,
the photograph shows the arrangement of a sample market usual
by the late nineteenth century.

Improved transport was the greatest single influence on these
changes, directing new trade to some markets and away from others.
The opening of the canal to Oxford brought the markets of that
county within easier reach of the urbanising Midlands. The markets
of such towns as Grantham and Newark were strengthened by the
coming of the railway which made contact with London more easy.

On the whole, improvements in transport had the effect of en-
hancing the standing of the larger corn markets at the expense of the
small ones. This trend was especially true of the railway's influence,
for it was now possible to make a journey which had taken a day on
horseback in two hours by train. This meant that the large markets
were able to attract buyers and sellers from further afield.

This is not to say that farmers and merchants never travelled far to
market before railways were built. Markets with any special attractions had always been able to draw people in, such as if a market was
especially noted for dealing in certain types of grain, thus making it
worth the farmer's while to take his samples to those dealers who

specialised in that grain. In Essex, Chelmsford was the market to attend for wheat, while Saffron Walden and Ware both had a reputation for dealing in barley. Similar divisions were found in most corn-growing counties. In Berkshire, Newbury was the wheat market; Reading and Abingdon were more important for barley.

The other main reason for covering long distances to market was that prices tended to be higher in the major markets. Prices in Norwich, by far the biggest corn market in Norfolk, were generally two or three shillings a quarter higher than those in King's Lynn or Bury St Edmunds. Markets on main roads offering easy access to London or the Midlands, such as Stamford, Lincoln, Newark and Gainsborough, were usually dearer than those in the more isolated parts of east Lincolnshire, at Spilsby or Louth, for example. The difference in prices between Lincoln and Louth was so great that at the beginning of the nineteenth century, farmers thought it worth while to take their barley the twenty-mile journey by road to Lincoln. They would set out about eight o'clock one evening, and not reach home again until about eight the following night.

The effect of railway travel was to cut out the overnight stops for such relatively short journeys, so that they could be made more regularly and frequently. Take the example of a farmer at Uffington at the western end of the Vale of the White Horse in Berkshire, whose diaries and accounts for the mid-nineteenth century survive. His nearest corn market was at Faringdon, five miles away, and his forebears had probably done most of their business there, selling to dealers who sold the grain on through the larger markets at Reading and Newbury to millers grinding for the London trade. With the train, the farmer could go to Newbury himself, a journey of twenty-five miles. This particular farmer travelled two or three times a week to Newbury, and rarely went to Faringdon to conduct market business.

The result of this increase in travel was that the smaller markets faded away. Faringdon itself, which had been of some note as a barley market for western Berkshire and eastern Wiltshire in the early eighteenth century, was reduced to a trifling trade by the late nineteenth century. It was luckier than the market at neighbouring Lambourn which, cut off from the main routes of nineteenth-century trade, ceased altogether. There were numerous similar examples up and down the country. Tuxford, in Nottinghamshire, was once an important staging point on the Great North Road, but, with East Retford and Newark within ten miles to north and south, the railway took its agricultural trade to those places, and Tuxford's market closed.

The railways did not always extinguish trade in the smaller markets, they could also revive a flagging trade. At Wantage, the corn market in the early nineteenth century was in the doldrums, its business transacted only 'between a limited number of neighbouring farmers and a few local dealers'. Efforts to revive trade, for instance by reducing tolls, were not proving successful. Although the Great Western Railway was not most conveniently sited for Wantage, passing some four miles to the north, the town's market authorities tried again to bring life to the corn trade. This time they succeeded in attracting dealers from Bristol, London and other main centres along the line of the railway, and soon the farmers decided it was worth while bringing their corn to Wantage. A small but important part of this revival was to move Wantage's market-day to Wednesday from the Saturday laid down in the ancient charter. This removed an element of direct competition with the larger market at Reading, held on Saturdays, and perhaps helped to entice some of the merchants to make Wantage a convenient Wednesday stop on their way to or from the major markets.

There were other places where similar revivals took place. Kirton Lindsey was a small town in Lincolnshire where life returned to a more or less defunct corn market after the railway to Gainsborough made the town more accessible. On the other hand, railway services could not create entirely new markets. A company attempted to promote corn trade at Didcot, the junction of the Great Western Railway's Oxford and Bristol lines. But the amount of corn passing through the market each week was enough to fill no more than three or four farm wagons. The established markets were far too strong.

All corn markets, however well established, felt the effects of agricultural depression in the last quarter of the nineteenth century. Arable farming was hit especially hard, and as the acreages under cereals fell, the trade passing through the corn exchanges declined drastically. A reduction in trade by as much as 75 per cent was not unusual. Berkshire's two largest markets, Newbury and Reading, had a trade in wheat of 49,000 quarters and 41,000 quarters respectively in 1851. In 1895 the quantity for both towns was about 13,500 quarters

25

of wheat, no more than one-third of that in 1851. Business at these two towns was dwarfed by the major eastern counties' markets, but trade was just as badly affected there. Boston was still handling more than 40,000 quarters of wheat in 1895, but that was only 20–25 per cent of the town's mid-century trade. Lincoln fared rather better than most places; trade in wheat did not fall quite so drastically, while an increase in the barley crop in the surrounding district was channelled through Lincoln's market.

Declining trade brought problems for the companies that had built the corn exchanges. Some were forced into liquidation, like the one at Loughborough which was made bankrupt in 1889. The corporation took over the exchange, but market business continued to decline, both from the effects of the depression, and from the fact that more transactions were made in other parts of town, at the cattle market, for example, during moments between viewing the animals. Even the market ordinary was not what it had been, being poorly attended, and the farmers were easily outnumbered by the corn merchants or other tradesmen of the town. Farmers simply could not afford to stay. As a 'stalwart old farmer of the old school' in Lincolnshire complained to a reporter in the 1890s, agricultural depression had made farmers 'hasten to catch early trains, instead of remaining for the afternoon to open port wine'.

LIVESTOCK FAIRS AND MARKETS

The fairs and markets for livestock present a wide variety. For just as some corn markets dealt mainly in wheat or barley, so there were specialisms among the sales for livestock, except that there were more different types of animal: cattle, sheep, pigs, horses, leanstock, fatstock, dairy cattle, young animals, the list seems endless. Most of the regular weekly markets dealt with at least cattle and sheep, and often pigs. Fatstock sales were commonly held on a different day of the week from the market for lean animals, and until the middle of the nineteenth century they were, like those at Lincoln and Skipton, held fortnightly rather than weekly.

It was the fairs that were most notable for specialising in a particular type of animal. Amongst those listed in Norfolk in the 1830s, there were fairs for cattle at Swaffham in July and November, and in May a sale for sheep as well. East Harling's May Fair was for cattle, with one for sheep in October. Aylsham held a fair on 25 March for lean cattle, but it was, as William Marshall found, 'chiefly noted for plow-horses, which at this season of the year become valuable to the Norfolk farmer, every hand and hoof becoming busily employed against barley seed time'. At the larger places there were further specialisations: Ipswich had lamb fairs of some renown, Lincoln held sales of rams and Horncastle had a horse fair of national, even international, fame. Even those fairs covering all types of stock often had a bias. Boston's May Fair was for both cattle and sheep, but it was the sheep that were the main attraction. This was a fair lasting two days, one day for sheep, the other for cattle. Lincoln's April Fair was organised in the same way, except that it lasted for four days, the first two days being for horses.

Aylsham fair was a small show. There were only about a hundred cattle on offer when William Marshall visited it, and nearly all the buying and selling was between farmers. Most of the fairs and quite a few of the markets were similar in covering mainly a local trade. The big sales were those attended by dealers involved in inter-regional trade. Skipton was the major market for Craven and the western dales of Yorkshire. At its leanstock markets there were cattle which had been brought across from the East Riding or from Scotland for sale to the graziers of Wharfedale and around Malham. Local breeders might have stock for sale to dealers taking cattle to markets in the Midlands. The fatstock markets attracted butchers from Manchester, Liverpool and most of the industrial towns of south-east Lancashire.

The biggest fairs, until the railway age, were those associated with the traffic mainly of lean cattle from Scotland, Wales and the north of England to the Midlands, East Anglia and the Home Counties, where they were fattened for the London market. The business of transferring the animals was the work of drovers who acted partly as dealers and partly as transport contractors. At one end of their routes were the fairs and markets, such as Falkirk, Aberaeron and Newcastle Emlyn, where the cattle were gathered together for the long trek south. At the other end were more big fairs - St Ives in Huntingdonshire, St Faith's at Norwich, Harlow Bush fair and Barnet - where the droves were disposed of. In between, were dozens of other markets and fairs, of various sizes, that the drovers attended to buy or to sell.

The major fairs were immense. Stagshaw Banks fair at Corbridge in Northumberland was where sheep from south-west Scotland were brought for sale to the farmers of north-east England. The numbers of sheep brought into the fair were reported to be over 100,000 at the end of the eighteenth century. Brough fair in Westmorland could have 10,000 head of cattle on view. At the other end of the drove routes, Barnet fair could attract 50,000 cattle, as well as a large show of sheep and horses brought for sale to London dealers. St Faith's fair, held on a hill just outside Norwich in mid-October, was of similar size. It officially lasted for three weeks, but sometimes went on longer if there were still cattle to sell; and there was a steady stream of cattle droves, some reported to be as large as 1,000 head, into the fair. Fields all round were used for accommodation of stock while the drovers tested the market with some of their herds.

Horse fairs provided more great occasions. Small sales were found at practically all market towns and not a few of the village fairs. Above those, however, were some fairs of regional and national renown. A number were to be found in the Midlands, Penkridge in Staffordshire holding one of the largest. Preston was important, as was Newcastle, but greatest of all were Howden and Horncastle, which attracted sellers and buyers from across the country. Reports vary as to which was the bigger of the two, so it is fair to assume that they were pretty well on a par.

The foundation of Horncastle's success was that it was in a strong horse-breeding county, although the horses at the fair were certainly not confined to the local supply. They were brought in from the Midlands and Ireland. Horses would be bought up at Newcastle to be sold again at Horncastle fair. Horncastle was internationally famous by the end of the eighteenth century. Despite being relatively out of the way, dealers were prepared to journey there by horse and by stage-coach from London and from as far across Europe as Hungary. Buyers from France, the Low Countries and Germany were particularly regular attenders. By the later nineteenth century there were even buyers from America, Australia and New Zealand. By then though, the fair was changing. It used to start in early August – nobody ever seemed sure of the official date, and it hardly mattered since trading tended to start almost as soon as people arrived at the town. The fair then lasted about two weeks, but it was reduced to one

Barnet Fair in 1849, a view from the *Illustrated London News*.

as the railway, opened in 1855, cut down the travelling times for buyer and seller. It also put an end to the work of the local equivalent of the Welsh cattle drover, the caddee, who used to take the horses away by road to their new homes.

Fairs like these were more than just business transactions, though. They were major spectacles bringing people from miles around to see the animals – especially the horses being put through their paces – and to amuse themselves at the side-shows. The poet Thomas Gray experienced this when he reached Brough in time for the fair in 1759. As he approached the town he saw:

'myriads of horses and cattle in the road itself and in all the fields round me ... thousands of clean healthy people in their best party-color'd apparel, farmers and their families, esquires and their daughters, hastening up from the dales and down the fells on every side, glittering in the sun and pressing forward to join the throng ... and the crowd (coming towards it) reach'd on as far as Appleby'.

The fairs were great social occasions. Even the smallest were times when families and friends, who perhaps did not see much of each other, came together for a gossip and a special meal. At the big fairs there might be a grand dinner attended by leading farmers and landowners, who were treated to two or three speeches on the state of the nation's agriculture. By contrast, Barnet fair was a gathering for the Welsh cattle drovers who organised their own games and races, while preachers came down from their chapels to hold special services.

The whole town was taken over by the big fairs. Those held in the town centre filled the streets, which were hardly less crowded where the fair's gathering was officially on a field outside the town. This was the arrangement at Barnet, yet, as a correspondent to the *Farmer's Magazine* in 1856 described, anyone wanting to go down the main streets of the town had to weave a path between droves of cattle being taken through the town either to or from the fair field. Passage along the pavements was obstructed by animals left tethered while those in charge of them were gathered in inns to settle payment for a deal and to drink part of the profit. The crowds were good for business generally in the town. The Lord of the Manor of Barnet tried to have the fair abolished, but was met with protests from the people of the town who claimed they would be ruined without the fair. By 1888, the fair had been altered by having a railway built across the middle of the field. As with the corn markets, the major effect of railways was to concentrate trade in some places at the expense of others, although there were numerous local variations in the pattern.

The movement of cattle over long distances was entrusted to the railways almost as soon as they opened. The drovers were quick to see that there was no point in wearing their animals out walking when they could be enjoying a ride, to arrive at the final markets fresher, healthier and worth more money. This in turn had deep effects on the cattle markets. Only a day or two was now needed to take cattle from Wales or Scotland to south-east England instead of three or four weeks' solid walking. The trains could deliver stock at frequent and regular intervals, and as a result, some of the fairs in Scottish and Welsh towns to gather stock together for the drive south became redundant, although those at larger towns such as Aberystwyth and Lampeter survived. The same happened in England. St Faith's fair declined as the business moved to Norwich's ordinary weekly markets. Dozens of small fairs in England disappeared as business was taken to larger markets. In Kent and Sussex the decline was especially

A small number of sheep and cattle crossing Eden Bridge on the
way to market at Carlisle.

dramatic, as railways broke through the isolation which had been
imposed by the terrain of the Weald. The number of places where
fairs took place in Kent, fell from 130 in 1792 to 13 in 1888, and in
Sussex the decline was from 119 to 41. Often a shadow of old fairs
lingered; farmers retained an attachment to old routines, not least
because of the social aspect of fair-day. So, although they might not
sell a single sheep, the farmers had a wonderful time meeting old
friends and relatives.

Barnet fair was still going strong in the 1880s. The protesters
against closure claimed that 50,000 head of cattle were still being
brought for sale. They may have exaggerated to reinforce their
argument, but other reports of the time comment on the size, the
bustle and excitement of the fair here. To some extent, perhaps
Barnet gained from the railways, in that instead of first meandering
round the markets of Leicestershire and Northamptonshire, the
Welsh drovers could load their stock on the train and come straight
to Barnet, Harlow and some of the other markets in Essex. Gradually, however, Barnet was changing character and becoming more of

a horse fair and pleasure fair. Reminiscences of the fair in about 1908 are of the great numbers of gypsies present, their horses decorated with ribbons and flowers. In the fun-fair were side-shows and round-abouts, while the gypsy women moved among the crowd selling lace, ribbons and clothes pegs.

Barnet was far from being alone in retaining a vigorous fair. Brough fair kept going, despite the railway from Appleby passing some miles outside the town. It was, though, reduced from two days to one, and it too, became increasingly a horse sale, in which form it survives today. Usually, the fairs were strongest in the towns with good railway services. The October Fair at Hereford achieved renown as the best to attend for that county's breed of cattle, and Horncastle's horse fair could attract buyers from the farthest continents. Even so, increasing competition came from the fair at Lincoln, which, unlike Horncastle, was not at the end of a small branch line.

It was not only ancient fairs which kept going during the nineteenth century. New ones were established, nearly all before 1850, and again it was at the towns best-served by rail that these had the best chance of success. Retford was one such place; a new fair was held in June 1840. The *Farmer's Magazine*, commenting favourably on its first showing, noted that buyers came from a wide area. Ten years later the town became a junction of two main railway lines, which helped ensure the continued success of the venture.

Railways had the same effects on the regular weekly cattle markets. The larger markets at towns with a good railway service attracted more business. In the 1840s Morpeth, one of the largest markets in the north-east, was visited regularly only by farmers living nearby. Its influence extended much further, but people coming from up to twenty miles away did so only occasionally. Thirty years later, Darlington was considered to be the principal market for farmers within a radius of thirty miles, while those at such places as North-allerton were confined to local business. Dorchester, in Dorset, was a town at the opposite end of the country to gain by the railway. By the 1860s, dealers were said to be coming regularly from most points along the Great Western main line. As important as the possession of a railway station to Dorchester's success though, was the opening in 1877 of a new cattle market on a field near the railway and away from the crowded main streets of the town.

The railways helped to change the nature of the cattle trade. Sales of fatstock increased, especially in the north where more stock was fattened locally instead of being sold to southern graziers. The local demand from the industrial towns was increasing, while the trains made light of the problem of getting perishable meat from northern Britain to London's Smithfield market. As fatstock sales became more frequent, new markets were set up, and not always in the old market towns. There was one at Crewe, a town created out of nothing by the railway with its important junction and locomotive works. In the late 1840s and 1850s the town equipped itself with agricultural markets. Cheese sales came first, for which an impressive market hall was built in 1854. Cattle fairs followed, five at first, but by 1858 there were ten every year. Then regular fatstock sales by auction were established in 1874, in a field behind the Royal Hotel, moving to a site near the railway station in 1882. Business built up quite quickly, the easy transport bringing buyers from the Potteries, Manchester and Birmingham. Meanwhile, older neighbours such as Nantwich and Sandbach found their trade harmed by the new market.

Until the middle of the nineteenth century, livestock markets were almost universally held in the centre of town. They might be in the market-place just a few yards away from the stallholders with their butter, eggs, vegetables and hardware. Alternatively, there might be a separate market-place a few streets away. King's Lynn was a large town with such an arrangement, Wetherby a small one. As the cattle markets outgrew their original accommodation, new market-places were laid out for them during the eighteenth and early nineteenth centuries. At Ipswich 'five public spirited individuals' paid £10,000 in 1809 for a new hall to accommodate the provisions market, and for a large space to be laid out for the livestock sales. Equally common was for the animals to be sold in one of the main streets of the town. Sheep pens were set up along each side of the street, while cattle were tethered to posts and railings. Horses might be sold at the same market. Chelmsford was one place where they were put through their paces for prospective buyers up and down the street outside the Saracen's Head inn.

Whichever the arrangement for the market, by the mid-nineteenth century accommodation in the town centre was becoming unsatisfactory. Space was a pressing problem for the farmers. At Hitchin in 1883, they complained of lack of space for the market held in one of

Market-day in Hereford *c.* 1898. The cattle market had been in a
reserved area to the north of the town since 1856, but animals
were still driven through the main streets.

the main streets, the problem being made worse by the opening of
new roads around the town centre and by the increasing number of
sheep being brought to market.

It was no less inconvenient for the citizens of a market town to
have the main streets filled with cattle, sheep and, for good measure,
the farmers' carts and their horses. Being market-day, the town was
crowded with shoppers, who found it difficult to move. The shopkeepers along the market street were none too pleased at the fact that
customers had to find a way between cattle to reach the shop door.
There were occasional less-expected problems, as when a bullock
being driven along Butcher's Row in Banbury took a fancy to a sweet
shop, and ambled round inside before crashing through the window
back out to the street. Then there were the complaints of the dirt and
smell, which became more frequent as consciousness of public clean-
liness spread. Even when they were not in the town, the cattle were no
more popular. At Chelmsford a particular bone of contention was
the number of holes made in the pavement along the High Street in
which tethering posts were erected. On days when there was no

The livestock market at Wellingborough *c*. 1900. This site was opened in 1875; the market was moved again in 1905.

market, people complained bitterly of stumbling over the postless holes.

A commonly adopted solution to these problems was to move the cattle and sheep out of the confines of the town centre to a new market-place. Shrewsbury was early to make the move, opening a new market in November 1850, and during the next twenty-five years or so, several other towns followed suit: Peterborough in 1866, Wellingborough in 1875. Some were the work of private enterprise, as at Retford opened in 1868; others were undertaken by the local authorities. The Local Board at Wellingborough spent £9,000 on the purchase of houses to be cleared for the site of the new market. These markets were nearly always sited as close to the railway as possible, occasionally, as at Retford, having a private siding and cattle dock. The move did not clear the streets entirely of cattle. Even in 1914, most stock walked to market and probably walked out of town again in the charge of a new owner, though the railway did carry those travelling more than five to ten miles. In the absence of bypass roads, a good proportion of the driven animals had to pass through the central streets.

Moving the cattle market was not always straightforward. In 1857, the surveyor at Hitchin had been asked to draw up a plan for a new market, but nothing came of it. Indeed, the Local Board of the town put off resiting the livestock, on the grounds of expense, until 1903 when national government ordered the market's removal. Slowness to make improvements was not unusual. At Colchester, the cattle market in the High Street was regarded as a 'foul blotch' by the 1850s, and a new site was a top priority for the borough council. Nonetheless, shortage of money and the difficulty of finding a new site delayed the move until 1863. It was not until the end of the 1870s that the people of Chelmsford could walk down their High Street without tripping over post holes. Meanwhile, the old farmers were grumbling about the unfamiliarity of the new market – 'you never know where to find anybody', they would say. Besides which, the White Hart and the Saracen's Head, where accounts had habitually been settled, were now a little walk from the market-place.

In 1892, while the Hitchin Local Board was busy doing nothing to improve the town's livestock market, sales of pigs were taking place in yards at the railway station, to which the Board took exception since it was losing the tolls that would have been charged if the animals had been brought to the official market. It might seem that the farmers and pig dealers were simply finding their own way out of the impossibly trying conditions in the street market. No doubt they were, but these sales were part of a more general trend towards private sales outside official markets, and it affected all towns whether their market-places were cramped or spacious. The Hereford October Fair was said in 1878 to be facing a decline in the numbers of cattle brought for sale because of the tendency to sell privately. There are similar reports from markets and fairs all round the country.

Private sales took a number of forms, one of these was by auction. The established markets were all based on private bargaining between seller and prospective buyer. If the farmer did not like what he was offered he could always take his animals home and bring them to another market. It was not uncommon for farmers to hawk their stock round the markets of two or three towns before they were satisfied with an offer. Auction sales were rare before the mid-nineteenth century, mainly because until 1845 they were subject to quite a heavy tax which made them hardly worth while. Once the tax

Crawley, Sussex, from a postcard of 1904. The streets are
crowded with cattle on the day of a fair.

was lifted, sale by auction began to become more popular. Most market towns had at least one auctioneer by the 1860s: there were four at Newbury and as many as twelve at Reading. While most auctioneers also undertook surveying, land agency and similar services, some followed less obvious occupations in conjunction with their auction sales. One at Newbury, for instance, was also a cabinet maker and upholsterer.

There were criticisms of auctions by those who thought they took away the farmer's skills of judgement, but the trend was the other way. Farmers felt they were getting a better price and a surer deal, and the buyers were similarly in favour. Auction marts for livestock were established at market towns everywhere, and attracted a high proportion of the trade. Some auctioneers worked within the established market, paying a due as licensed traders, rather more set up their own private markets in a yard or on a piece of waste ground around the town. The bigger firms had properly equipped auction rooms. Mr Robinson Mitchell, for instance, established the Agricultural Hall in Cockermouth, which by 1874 had an annual turnover of nearly 10,000 cattle and 40,000 to 50,000 sheep.

The second form of private sale took the business out of the market town altogether and on to the farm. Sometimes there might be a special auction at the farm, a practice favoured especially by breeders of pedigree livestock. Farmers also sold animals in ones and twos to the local butcher or to dealers who would regularly pay a visit. There was nothing new about this type of trading; it just became more common in the late nineteenth century – common enough to have an appreciable effect on the numbers of animals passing through regular markets. Ultimately the extension of this practice, together with transport by motor lorry, was to bring about the demise of many small markets.

=2=
Commercial Life

MARKETS AND FAIRS

The retail market was perhaps the liveliest part of town on market day, for here was the greatest variety of traders and customers. Everything was sold from food and cooking utensils for the home to new ploughs for the farm. A mid-nineteenth century description of Yarmouth market-place describes the typical scene:

'The long rows of stalls stretch out further than anyone can see, and we may pass from the display of fish, flesh, and fowl at one end, through peas and potatoes, cakes and strawberries, to baskets, bedsteads, boxes, boots, frippery, old iron and new hardware, old chairs, and old books. There sits a busy knife-grinder, whirling off a hissing stream of sparks amid an admiring group. There the dealer in literature disperses odd volumes to rural shelves, and announces that he is ready to buy as well as to sell ... Some of the stalls are roofed, but most are uncovered, and near each there is a small sentry box, in which the women can sit sheltered from sun and rain while selling their poultry, butter, or vegetables. The lover of floral beauty will soon permit his eye to rest on the produce of the market garden, where it may revel in a perfect sea of lusciousness ...'

Celia Fiennes, who made a tour of England at the end of the seventeenth century, commented on the wide variety of goods on sale in the markets through which she passed, and Doncaster market was described by Clifton Johnson in the 1890s, as just as much a hurly-burly as Yarmouth in the 1860s. However, the impression that the general street markets and fairs were the same from one century to the next is deceptive. The eighteenth and nineteenth centuries in fact saw some substantial changes in the character and organisation of

39

these markets.

One of the greatest changes was the demise of the general fairs, or great marts as they were otherwise called. These fairs, held mostly in spring and autumn had, since medieval times, been important as a means of distributing foods and manufactured goods throughout the country. The people of the town and its surrounding villages were able to buy many of their domestic needs retail at these fairs, but their greater function was in wholesale distribution. Shopkeepers came to buy their stock for the next six months or a year from the merchants who took their wares around the fairs. Institutions, such as colleges, and some of the houses of great landowners with large domestic establishments would also use the fairs to stock up on household needs.

General fairs were held in all the towns of the country and in several villages, especially those which had failed to develop into towns in past ages. Usually a wide range of goods was on offer, but there were fairs noted for certain articles. Chester held fairs in July and October which were probably the most important in the country for Irish linen, and attracted buyers from all corners. The merchants of Manchester and Yorkshire brought their cotton goods to these fairs, to be sold in buildings 'conveniently fitted up for the purpose', these being two cloth halls built in 1778 and 1809. Two other towns in Cheshire, Macclesfield and Northwich, featured the cloth of Manchester and the West Riding at their fairs, but these were not on the scale of Chester's.

Sturbridge fair, held in a field outside Cambridge, was probably the largest general fair in the country in the early eighteenth century, able to stand comparison, thought Daniel Defoe, with the greatest continental fairs such as Nuremburg and Leipzig. Sturbridge had clearly defined retail and wholesale sections. The retail section was made up of streets of stalls, even bearing street names such as Cheapside. There were stallholders, mainly from London, of almost every description: hatters, haberdashers, drapers, jewellers, toymakers and turners. Shoppers could find refreshment at the numerous coffee-houses, brandy shops and eating-houses. The wholesale trade was housed in larger marquees where the dealers met and bargained. The commodities most prominent at Sturbridge when Daniel Defoe investigated the fair were hops, wool and cloth. Hops were brought up from Kent, Farnham and the Chelmsford area of

Essex, at that time a district where hops were grown in reasonable quantity, to be sold to buyers from all over central and northern England. The cloth trade came mainly from the opposite direction. Clothiers came down from Halifax, Leeds and Huddersfield with Yorkshire woollen cloth, and from Lancashire with cotton goods. There were Devonshire merchants offering serges, shalloons and kerseys. Sacking, blankets and quilts were brought from Kidderminster, and woollen cloth from Norwich. All these were principally for sale to dealers from London and the south-east. The wool trade was in the long wools of Lincolnshire, which were bought by the manufacturers of East Anglia. Defoe reported that sales of wool could reach £50,000 to £60,000 in value.

Sturbridge fair was probably at or near its peak in Defoe's time, for by the end of the eighteenth century its trade had fallen off considerably. Improved transport was the principal cause for the decline of Sturbridge and other general fairs. Roads in 1800 were in better condition than they had been in 1720, and canals had been built. It was no longer so important for London wholesalers to go out to Cambridge once a year to meet clothiers from Leeds. They, or their agents, could meet more frequently in one another's home districts to transact business. Deliveries of goods could be made more reliably in regular lots throughout the year, so shopkeepers had less need to stock up for months ahead at fair time. What finally killed general fairs off was the railways, which cut through the remaining obstacles to the speedy and frequent distribution of goods.

By 1850, the fairs were well on the wane. The experience of the great mart at King's Lynn, which formerly lasted for six days from 13 February, was typical. In 1849, the *Norwich Mercury* reported that

'in days of yore this mart was considered one of the largest trading fairs ... and was the resort of traders from all parts of the kingdom, who supplied the inhabitants far and near with every description of goods, useful and ornamental, but of late years its trading character has sunk into comparative insignificance and it is now nothing more than a pleasure fair'.

There had often been side-shows and amusements at these fairs and, as the trading side declined, it was common for the fun-fair to take over. This was often unpopular with the respectable citizens of

Victorian towns who complained that the fairs promoted indecorous and criminal behaviour. Stricter controls were therefore necessary. Shopkeepers were among the supporters of such moves. At Banbury, the shops had traditionally had their business limited for the duration of the Michaelmas Fair, mainly because stalls blocked their entrances. That was accepted while the fair had a trading function, but as that declined the shopkeepers argued that they could provide all the goods the fair had done and with less boisterous behaviour. The retailers of Bury St Edmunds put forward those arguments in a petition to the town council in 1858 that the fair should be discontinued. The petitioners were unsuccessful on this occasion, but several fairs were suppressed as public nuisances. The one at Harwich was stopped in 1857 and Sudbury's had been abandoned by 1860.

Improved transport had a similar effect on some of the specialised fairs dealing in agricultural produce, such as butter, cheese and wool. The greater regularity of supply meant that trade need no longer be conducted through fairs. The Michaelmas Fair at Reading had been one of the biggest in the country for cheese. Supplies from the main cheese-making districts of the West Country came here for sale to merchants from London and the southern and midland counties. In the late eighteenth century, business was considerable: 1,200 tons were sold in 1795. After that, decline set in, hastened by the arrival of the railway, when, according to the *Reading Mercury*, sales were 'effected to a very considerable extent without the commodity being brought into the fair. A good deal was left unloaded in the railway and sold by sample'. Reading's cheese fair disappeared, but others kept going, especially in towns in and around the producing districts. The cheese fair at Whitchurch, Shropshire, was still active in 1890. The pitch of thirty-five tons was regarded as good, and, reported *Bell's Weekly Messenger*, there was a good demand for coloured cheese, 'which went off well'. The pattern was complicated again by the fact that, as well as taking trade away from some fairs, the existence of railway transport encouraged merchants in some places to start new fairs, and a number of these became successfully established.

The traditional part of the market town's trading activities that proved the most resilient and adaptable was the weekly retail market. It was subject to the same pressures as the fairs: the more rapid distribution of goods through improved transport, competition from permanent shops, and competition from the products of new

People arriving with their fruit and vegetables to sell round the
market cross. A drawing by W.H. Pyne published in 1806.

industries which tended to be sold through these shops. There were
numbers of ancient markets which fell casualty to those pressures and
especially to the widening sphere of influence of the larger markets.
Thus, the small market of Bingham in Nottinghamshire faded away
as the railways took its customers to Nottingham. In Derbyshire all
that remained of the once-flourishing market at Tideswell in the early
years of the present century was one solitary seller of pottery in the
market-place.

However, despite the competition from shops, the retail market
continued to hold its own as the supplier of cheap food and manufactured goods. The poor were the mainstay of the trade, though
farmers, gentry and wealthy townspeople did some of their shopping
in the market by sending their servants to make the purchases. The
value of the market is demonstrated best by the keenness of new
industrial towns to emulate their older country cousins by establishing their own markets. Burslem, in the Potteries, obtained the right
to hold a market by Act of Parliament in 1825, and built a covered
market hall in 1835. By the end of the century, large numbers of
industrial towns, such as Accrington in Lancashire, Stalybridge in
Cheshire and Clay Cross in Derbyshire, possessed markets which did

not exist a hundred years before.

In order to survive, the retail market's character changed in a number of ways. Its main strength was in the supply of cheap food, and the trend was for its trade to be concentrated in this area as shops increasingly provided effective competition in clothing, pottery, wooden turned ware, basketry and many other types of domestic hardware. The eighteenth-century market had covered a wide range of goods, but by the 1850s most of the stallholders were selling food. A survey of Leicester market in 1851 showed that seventy-nine per cent of the stalls were selling food. Drapery and clothing was often the second largest part of the later nineteenth-century market, with household goods represented to a varying degree from place to place.

Even the food market was not all-embracing. Bakers were generally shopkeepers by the late eighteenth century. William Marshall remarked on it as unusual to see cart-loads of country bread on sale in the market when he visited Bideford in 1794, and in the survey of Leicester there was just one baker's stall. Butchers, on the other hand, were numerous – by far the largest single trade in Leicester market-place. They had traditionally been an important part of the market, and a special building, the shambles, was often provided where butchers from the villages had their stalls and could slaughter and butcher meat on the spot. At Lincoln a new hall, the Butchery, was built in 1774, and twenty-eight butchers from villages within a radius of ten miles had their pitches here in the 1850s. The tradition was continued in the new market hall built at Barnstaple in the 1880s which included a butchers' row with thirty-three shops.

In several other towns the trend had been for butchers to move out of the market-place to better permanent shops. Concern for public health was also producing movements to clean up the towns, and one of the targets was the shambles. The old buildings were swept away either to be replaced by a new market hall or to give more room for the open stalls, leaving the butchers to find new homes. Pickering was one town to make this move, demolishing the shambles, which had housed six butchers' stalls, in 1857, and in Hitchin the shambles were removed from the market-place in 1856. A principal reason was that the old buildings obscured the view of the corn exchange, which had just cost the town £2,600 to build, though a glance at photographs of the 1850s suggests the move had ample justification, since the word shambles could be applied to the buildings in its more modern sense.

The market cross at Ipswich in 1773. To its right are the
shambles where the butchers set up their stalls under the
open galleries of the ground floor.

The shambles in Hitchin, in common with those at several other
towns, had by 1850 ceased to be occupied exclusively by butchers.

One of the features of the general market was the number of casual
sellers. Farmers' wives were the largest part of this body, as they
would bring in butter, poultry, eggs and fruit as they happened to
have produce available. They brought their wares to town usually in
great baskets, from which in Devon the trade gained the name
'pannier market'. Some markets had what was known as pitching
sales, where sellers did not have stalls, but simply spread their wares
on the ground. Ipswich was one to have that tradition, so was
Grantham, though by the 1880s it was restricted to a small area for
sellers of pots. The trend was, though, for these parts of the market
to decline and for a greater proportion of the trade to be in the hands
of professional stallholders.

Similarly, the numbers of craftsmen who sold their own products
of such things as pottery or wooden ware declined, leaving the trade
in the hands of those who were retailers only. The change was far
from complete by 1914. The pannier market in such towns as

Barnstaple continued to flourish for many years beyond that, helped by a healthy passing trade from tourists for butter, cream and eggs.

Among the sellers at markets and fairs were the itinerant cheapjacks and hawkers. Cheapjacks were few in number and represented the upper end of this world of business, travelling round with pony and cart selling Birmingham and Sheffield ware: pocket knives, cutlery, bridles, whips, padlocks and other light items of hardware. The anonymous memoirs of a cheapjack, published in 1876, record the type of itinerary that might be undertaken. Setting out from London, he attended Romford market on Wednesday, Bishops Stortford Thursday, on Friday Chelmsford, and Saturday Colchester. Going on through Suffolk and Norfolk, he reached Diss the following Thursday and Norwich on Saturday.

Most of the itinerants at markets were petty hawkers who tramped round with packs full of cheap crockery, thimbles, song sheets and the like, which they would offer to the public through an elaborate patter, giving more value in terms of entertainment than through the quality of their goods. To some extent, the railways helped the itinerants, widening the circuits they could cover from their bases in the cities. In the longer term, though, the railways built up the competition for the hawkers, by bringing supplies to the cheap 'fancy goods' shop of the country town. By the 1870s, the itinerants were disappearing from the market-places.

In contrast with agricultural markets where the business was concentrated into a few hours, the general market was commonly open all day, and in some places continued late into the evening. At Nottingham the market lasted until 11 p.m., lit by naphtha flares attached to the stalls. Long trading hours met the needs of customers who might have had difficulty finding time free to visit the markets. Evening markets, especially, were found in towns with plenty of industries, whose factory workers would be working long, fixed hours. This also helped make Saturday the most popular market-day. Ilkeston, in Derbyshire, was one of several towns where the market-day was moved to Saturday during the late nineteenth century; Mansfield added a Saturday market to the Thursday of its charter. Eastwood, in a rapidly industrialising part of Nottinghamshire, was an exception. The Saturday market was abandoned in favour of one on Friday evening as the only means of competing with the far larger markets at Nottingham.

The Market Place, Shrewsbury; an engraving of 1845.
The small scale of trade shown is almost entirely conducted
by sellers pitching their wares on the ground.

In common with other parts of the market town's trade, such as
the corn and cattle markets, accommodation for the retail market was
improved. During the late eighteenth century there was widespread
concern that the existing market-places were proving inadequate,
with cramped accommodation for stallholders around market
crosses, underneath town halls and around the main streets. Schemes
for improvement were put forward, increasing in number and scope
as Victorian urban redevelopment got under way. Improvements to
markets ranged from repaving the market-place and rearranging the
stalls more efficiently to avoid traffic congestion, to the building of
new covered market halls. Covered markets were a feature mainly of
northern and midland towns. They were built first in industrial
centres, and the idea spread to nearby country towns. They were not
always a complete success, though. At Bridgnorth, the stalls for the
market on Saturday were set out in the High Street and under the old
market house while the new hall, built in 1855, was used for offices
and store rooms. Lincoln and Bishop Auckland were two towns
where covered markets were built, but with open sides, with the
result that though the market population might stay dry, they caught
the full blast of any wind.

HIRING FAIRS

Hiring fairs, known otherwise as mops or statute fairs, went into decline during the second half of the nineteenth century, due mainly to changing social attitudes and practices. These were the fairs held for farmers to engage farm workers and domestic servants for a term usually of a year, sometimes six months. The fairs had been held in market towns since medieval times. The name 'statute' was derived from the Statute of Labourers, a law passed during the reign of Richard II to regulate the terms and conditions of employment. The practice of hiring labour through fairs though, went back far beyond its incorporation into King Richard's law.

Nearly all annual hirings were made either at May Day or in the autumn between Michaelmas and Martinmas, and at those seasons there was a succession of statute fairs. Labourers and servant girls offering themselves for employment would stand around the market-place or high street in groups. They dressed up in their best clothes and often wore or carried with them some indication of the type of work they were seeking. Carters might wear a piece of whipcord twisted round their hats, shepherds wore a piece of wool around their hats or carried their crooks, while servant girls might carry a broom. Bearing marks of their trade was not the universal practice; at Ulverston any man for hire simply had a matchstick stuck in his hat.

The farmers and their wives walked around the groups of workers, looking them over. The process was mutual, as those seeking work studied the farmers and their wives, since the standard of fare at meals was a prime factor in the decision to accept or reject offered employment. While they were waiting for offers, the labourers would compare notes about past experiences on the different farms. When he had spotted a likely-looking person, the farmer would approach and discuss the terms of employment, perhaps over a cup of tea and a cake at a nearby shop. The bargaining could be hard, since the terms agreed depended on the strengths of supply and demand, which all could see simply by looking around at the numbers who had come to the fair.

When the terms had been settled, the bargain was sealed by the farmer handing the man a 'fastening penny'. Inflation since Richard II's time meant that the penny was, in fact, usually sixpence or a

The crowded scene of a hiring fair at Burford c. 1905.

shilling, even, by 1914, half a crown. The system was not completely free from abuse, since there were the occasional unscrupulous men who cheerfully accepted the shilling, then went back into the market-place to hire themselves to another farmer.

With a succession of fairs in neighbouring towns, it was common for those who failed to get a position at one to move on and try their luck at the next. Thus, Lancaster statutes were on Martinmas Saturday, and those unsuccessful there moved on to Ulverston for the following weekend. However, by the 1870s the practice of hiring labour at special fairs was breaking down. Reports in newspapers and the observations of such commentators as Richard Jefferies, generally agreed that the business at hiring fairs was becoming less brisk as the years passed. Employment for the term of a year was becoming less popular, both for the workers who wanted the greater flexibility to move which being employed from week to week allowed, and for the farmers who began to regard having labourers boarded at the farmhouse as an unnecessary domestic burden. There were other satisfactory ways of finding employment, in particular advertisements in newspapers, which were open to more people as the standard of literacy improved. Moreover, engagements made through this medium did not have to be restricted by the dates of the fairs.

Despite the competition it faced, the traditional hiring fair took some time to disappear. Even in southern counties of England, where the practice of annual hiring had been declining since at least the beginning of the nineteenth century, there were fairs active into the 1890s. Newbury's was one of these, having a particularly busy year in 1890. Lincoln statutes could still attract 200 to 300 men seeking work in 1900; indeed this fair and at least two dozen others continued to be used for hiring beyond 1918. The decline of hiring did not mean the end of the fair: it became a fun-fair. There always had been entertainments at which many a fastening penny was spent. This part of the day's activities tended to grow and take over from the former business. Many of today's pleasure fairs are the survivals of the old statutes.

SHOPS AND SHOPPING

The market town's retailing and service trades were in large measure directed towards the surrounding countryside. In Thomas Hardy's description of Dorchester in its guise as Casterbridge, this connection was shown

'by the class of objects displayed in the shop windows. Scythes, reap-hooks, sheep-shears, bill-hooks, spades, mattocks, and hoes at the ironmonger's; bee-hives, butter-firkins, churns, milking stools and pails, hayrakes, field-flagons, and seedlips at the cooper's; cart-ropes and plough-harness at the saddler's; carts, wheelbarrows, and mill-gear at the wheelwright's and machinist's; horse-embrocations at the chemist's; at the glover's and the leather cutter's hedging gloves, thatchers' knee caps, ploughmen's leggings, villager's pattens and clogs.'

Meeting the needs of the farming world remained an important part of the town's services throughout the nineteenth and early twentieth centuries. On market-days shopkeepers used to put an extra display of goods outside the shop to attract the farmers. At Bungay in Suffolk, the local ironfounder and plough dealer had a

Saddlers Row, Petworth, in 1905. A saddler's shop was
still to be found; Pellett's, formerly a grocery, was now
a stationer and tobacconist.

show of farm implements in the market-place, a feature which was
also found in other towns, such as Hitchin in Hertfordshire.

However strong the farmers' demand though, retailing in the
market towns increasingly moved towards selling a wider range of
general consumer goods, all the products of the industrial revolution.
In all towns with a strong market area, a shopping centre developed
containing more and bigger shops. As with many other features of the
market towns' story, the weaker places dropped behind.

One of the features of retailing in the country town to decline as
competition from shops grew, was the travelling salesman. There
were two distinct types of traveller. One visited the town from
outside. Of this type, the cheapjacks and hawkers, who attended the
markets and fairs, have already been met. A higher class version of the
same type of selling is represented by John Richardson from London
who advertised in *Jackson's Oxford Journal* in October 1762 that he
would shortly be staying at Mr Cock's on the Bridge at Abingdon for
one week, where he would be selling wholesale and retail silks, Irish
linens and other quality drapery.

Apart from those were the local country travellers, tradesmen
who, said Daniel Defoe, 'do also keep shops or chambers, or ware-

houses in the adjacent market towns, and sell their goods in the villages round'. Theirs was one of the oldest methods of retailing and, though declining from about the 1860s, continued to have some part in country trade until the end of the nineteenth century. The most substantial of the itinerants were the travelling or pack drapers. Directories for the mid-nineteenth century mention one or two in most of the larger market towns, and their entries continue to appear, though in fewer numbers, in succeeding editions. There were two at Newbury in the directory for 1895, for example. Pack drapers sold cheap cloth and clothing to the cottage dwellers, calling from door to door. They had, wrote Richard Jefferies, 'no shop window, and make no display, but employ several men carrying packs, who work through the villages on foot, and range over a wide stretch of country'.

A few others amongst the travellers gained the respectability of an entry in the trades directory. There were some travelling tea dealers, for instance, at Spalding. There were others whose main business was a shop in the town, but as a sideline did some door to door selling around the villages. Flora Thompson recalled one who visited Lark Rise in the 1880s selling furniture, and for a while did quite a brisk trade in washstands and baths sold on hire-purchase. Most of the itinerants, however, were humble pedlars and tinkers whose base in the towns was far smaller than the shops and warehouses listed in directories. The pedlars came out to the villages selling small items to the poor cottagers, such as needles and thread, matches and small toys for the children. Tinkers had their barrows with a grindstone and tools for sharpening knives and mending pots and pans.

Retailing in the eighteenth-century country town was little removed from manufacturing. Most shops were workshops occupied by craftsmen who made nearly all of the goods they sold. Abingdon, a fair-sized town in the 1790s with about 4,300 inhabitants, had just four people described as shopkeepers. Another six were grocers, at least one of whom divided his time with another business. These were the general retailers of the town, selling a wide range of food and household items, such as tea, sugar, candles and string. There was a clear distinction between those who were selling to the poor and those catering for the middle classes and gentry. For the latter, success in the business depended upon the quality of service offered, which meant meeting individual tastes, arranging for purchases to be delivered and attending to such details as the neatness with which parcels were wrapped. Whoever he was selling to though, the shop-keeper did not simply sell goods exactly as he had bought them. It was usual for him to make up his own blends of tea, his own mixtures of spices, to cure bacon and grind coffee. Even such things as sugar did not reach the shop in individual packets, but had to be weighed out into quarter-pound, half-pound and one pound lots to suit each customer.

What was true of the grocers was also true of most other retailers. They did more than just sell things. The bakers made their bread, the butchers killed the animals and jointed them. The clothing trades were clearly in the hands of producer-retailers; those listed in Abing-don's directory were all tailors, breeches-makers and hat-makers. There were makers of gloves, stays and perukes, the wigs which were fashionable in the eighteenth century. All of these were seeking the custom of the farmers, gentry and wealthy townsmen. When the poor bought, or had mended, clothes, they went to the seamstresses who lived and worked in the back streets and alleys. Amongst all the retail trades, the principal ones that could be counted as straightfor-ward shopkeepers in the modern sense were the drapers and haber-dashers, whose involvement with the goods they sold was perforce confined to cutting cloth or ribbons to the required length. Abing-don had about six of these shops in the 1790s. There were a few smaller trades which were purely retail, such as the brandy merchant and the man listed as a chinaman, referring not to his origins but to the fact that he sold high-class crockery.

During the course of the nineteenth century, the shopkeepers of the market town became more purely retailers, less involved in packaging and manufacturing the goods they sold. The drapery and grocery trades led the way in this transformation, and by the 1860s the style of marketing was changing. Shops were becoming larger and stocking a wider range of goods. John Evans of Abingdon described his business in the 1860s as cabinet-maker, upholsterer, dealer in all sorts of bedroom ware, clothes boxes, carpeting and matting, and added 'there are six large showrooms behind the shop.'

The rate at which retailing changed increased from about 1870. Mechanisation had been expanding rapidly into a number of con-sumer industries so that now large-scale manufacturers and whole-salers were able to supply cheap, ready-made clothes, and food made

The butcher's shop of W. Smith & Sons in Market Street,
Aylesbury, in 1908.

up in small packets. These firms were also meeting a demand from the
lower middle and working classes, whose real incomes were rising,
and who were ready to buy ready-made and packaged goods that were
not too expensive. Grocers' shops in the country towns were now
stocked with pickles and sauces, meat, vegetables, biscuits, chocolate
and cocoa, lampblack and washing blue, all supplied by the manufacturers and wholesalers in boxes, tins and bottles.

The clothing and household trades were similarly affected. Mass-
produced furniture came from London and High Wycombe at a
fraction of the cost for which the local cabinet-maker could make the
items. By the 1860s there were factories in Norwich and Northampton with steam-driven sewing machines, each one of which could turn
out 600 pairs of shoes a day. The boot and shoemaker of the market
town came to stock ready-made goods to meet his basic trade, only
making shoes himself for the upper end of the market. Mechanisation
came later to the clothing factories, but by the 1890s cheap, ready-
made suits were available everywhere. Even such craftsmen as the

Borough Stores – G. Burgess's grocery and meat business in
Godalming, photographed probably in the 1890s.

saddler were now stocking saddles and harnesses which had been
either wholly or partly manufactured in factories in the West
Midlands.

The nature of the shops also changed. The shopkeepers of the
1790s had had little workshops opening directly on to the street, with
a small display of their wares on view. Wooden shutters were pulled
down when the shop was closed for the night. Shops of the nineteenth century were fronted with plate glass windows, and, as mass
marketing developed, these were filled with displays and advertisements for prominent branded goods, such as Fry's cocoa or Sunlight
soap. Shops selling furniture and cheap drapery did not stop at bold
window displays in the unrestrained years before the First World
War; letters a foot high on whitewashed walls would proclaim the
bargains to be had from the store.

The changes in retailing tended to turn the two or three central
streets in the town more exclusively into shopping areas. Inns and
banks would remain amongst the shops, but craftsmen and wholesale

dealers moved out to be replaced by retailers. At Abingdon people such as the bricklayer, the brush-maker, three hat manufacturers, two slop sellers and a monumental mason, who all had premises in the High Street in the 1820s, had gone by the 1890s. Among those who came in their place were the Post Office, a china and glass dealer, a photographer and a tobacconist. In small towns where commerce was hardly expanding this turnover was slower and less complete. Winslow, in Buckinghamshire, with no more than 1,704 inhabitants in 1891, still had a blacksmith in the market square, and along the High Street there were two builders' yards and a cooper's premises.

New types of shop came to the main streets. In the North, co-operative societies spread out from their original bases in the industrial towns into even the smallest country towns. There was, for example, a society in Allendale, a Northumberland town which had lost its markets by the late nineteenth century. The societies were usually small, confined to one town only, although there were exceptions, especially in districts where industry was growing up. Ripley, in Derbyshire, was a thriving market town whose life was being taken over during the late nineteenth century by the ironworks of the Butterley Company. There was a successful co-operative society which also had branches in Alfreton and Codnor, two other places within the influence of expanding coal-mines. The establishment of branch shops, however, was generally brought to market towns by a new breed of multiple retailing businesses in the 1880s and 1890s.

Multiple retailers can trace their history back to the railway bookstalls of W.H. Smith which were opened in the late 1840s, while some grocery businesses in the large cities established branch shops in the mid-nineteenth century. It was not until the 1870s and 1880s, however, that large regional and national chains were built up by such firms as the International Tea Company, the London Central Meat Company and the shoe sellers Freeman, Hardy & Willis. Boots Cash Chemists, selling soaps and basic medicines at about half the prices charged by smaller firms, spread across the east Midlands during the 1880s and 1890s. By 1914, with 560 branches, the company was approaching national coverage.

In common with other retailing chains, Boots went to the larger towns first. In Norfolk in 1912, where the firm was a relative newcomer, there were shops only at Norwich, King's Lynn and

Godalming, Surrey, early this century. The spread of
nationally distributed goods such as Fry's chocolate
is indicated, while agricultural business is still
attended to by the forage contractor.

Yarmouth. The importance of these places in the eyes of Boots management was great enough for there to be as many as five branches in Norwich and three in Yarmouth. The small towns were left with few representatives of multiple retailers, only half a dozen at Diss for example, but that was twice as many as twenty years previously. For towns like Yarmouth, where by 1912 there were branches of chains ranging from Boots to Maypole Dairy, Hepworths the outfitters and Marks & Spencer's bazaar, the new stores could only enhance their standing as shopping centres. This was especially true for the popular mass consumption items, advertised nationally – Boots, for one, used the new press, such as the *Daily Mail*, to promote its bargains.

Meanwhile, some of the independent traders of the market towns had been building up little business empires. The drapers usually led the way, adding a few new lines to their stock every so often until by the end of the century they had become department stores, in which guise many still exist, though not always as independent businesses. They were followed by furniture dealers, who extended the range of goods they would stock, and by such shops as chandlers, stationers and fancy goods dealers, who moved into different lines until they became a form of general store. The process was at work early in the nineteenth century. In 1791 Charles Heath had set up shop as bookseller and printer in Monmouth; when he died in 1833 his business was also selling tea, patent medicines and perfume.

In the second half of the nineteenth century the changes were on a larger scale. Shops grew in size by taking over neighbouring premises or by moving to a new site. By 1907, Watts's furniture store, which had started as a small shop in Northampton, was advertising its 7,000 square feet showrooms. The next step in expansion was to rebuild the store, providing the business with a handsome new building which would be more prominent in the high street. Some market town firms had two or three branches. Footman & Co., a Suffolk drapery business, had shops in Woodbridge, Stowmarket, Ipswich and Braintree by 1883. It was not always the biggest businesses nor those in the larger market towns that expanded into branch shops. William Lacey's business in Lincolnshire was probably dwarfed by the major stores of Lincoln or Boston, but in the 1890s he had drapery shops in the small towns of Wainfleet, Alford and Winterton.

CHAMBERLIN, SONS, & CO.,

SILK MERCERS,

MANTLE & COSTUME MAKERS,

Linen and Woollen Drapers,

HABERDASHERS, CARPET FACTORS,

AND

WHOLESALE CLOTHIERS AND MANCHESTER WAREHOUSEMEN,

Importers of French and other Continental Manufactures.

FAMILY MOURNING.

NORWICH.

One of the large stores of the bigger towns in the late nineteenth
century; from an advertisement of 1883.

COMMERCIAL AND PROFESSIONAL SERVICES

One of the features of the market town was its inns and public houses. Towns such as Salisbury and Newark had been noted in earlier centuries for the number and quality of their inns. Throughout the period covered in this book, inns continued to offer a variety of services to the residents and visitors to country towns. A few have been noticed already: the inns acting as market-place, warehouse and stable, and meeting place for relaxation when market business was completed. The licensed trade was heterogeneous, ranging from the major commercial and posting inns, and the respectable establishments patronised by the gentry for their social and political gatherings to the small beerhouses where labouring folk came to drink, and play music and games.

Inns and public houses were to be found in large numbers in market towns. There was a tavern to every hundred people in Abingdon in 1830, a ratio that was not unusual. Bewdley's eighty-seven licensed houses in 1854 represented one for every forty-two inhabitants, although in parts of London the balance was tipped even more in favour of the public house. Such disproportionate numbers seem quite remarkable, but, as has been suggested, the country town inn was more than just a drinking establishment. The inn was catering for visitors and the numbers to some extent represented potential peak demand. Every house in Horncastle was packed to overflowing for the few weeks of the August horse fair, when during the rest of the year there may well have been more than enough inns for the town. Indeed at fair times, there could be temporary additions to the numbers of taverns. Special 'bush' licenses, costing five shillings, could be bought by any householder, allowing him to sell beer for the period of the fair. He had to display a bush, or a branch or two, as a temporary inn sign.

Innkeeping was often a part-time occupation, possibly because the large number of inns meant they were not especially profitable. Whatever the reason, it was not at all unusual for licensees to have another occupation, farming or market gardening being a common one. Less usual was Mr Humphris, the publican at the Swan, Banbury, early in the nineteenth century. He also had extensive gardens where he grew roses for use in medicines. Other publicans

The Crown Hotel, Wells, Somerset. The late seventeenth-century building looks a little the worse for wear in this view taken around 1900. The importance of the large brewers in Burton upon Trent is attested by the signs on the windows.

were shopkeepers, butchers and craftsmen with businesses in the town, others were carriers and a few had small manufacturing businesses: another of Banbury's licensees was a plush manufacturer.

From the 1870s, stricter licensing, a decline in the sales of beer and the strength of the temperance movement combined to bring about a reduction in the number of public houses. The fifty-two licensed premises in Abingdon in 1830 had been reduced to thirty-seven by 1895, while in Bewdley the decline was even more steep, to twenty-two in 1892. Sometimes these losses were offset a little by the opening of temperance hotels, but there were rarely more than a couple in any town.

Professional and commercial services expanded, even in towns of modest size and limited markets. By the end of the nineteenth century there were more doctors, dentists and vets; there were piano-tuners and teachers of music, and more lawyers and land agents. Accountancy as a separate occupation had not existed at the beginning of the nineteenth century; by its end, there were as many as eight firms in Reading, and one or two in the smaller towns such as

Wallingford and Hungerford. There were insurance offices in 1800, and they increased in number over the next few decades. By 1856 there were as many as twenty-four firms in Horncastle competing for business from the town's 5,000 inhabitants. Falling population and the combination of insurance companies into larger firms brought that figure down to seven by the 1890s. Newbury similarly had fewer insurance offices as firms like the Commercial Union moved in to replace smaller businesses such as the Hampshire Sussex and Dorset fire office.

The development of these services in market towns reflected the growing complexities of trade in the countryside and a rise in the standard of living over the nineteenth century. The legal profession had been growing in numbers and influence in country towns during the eighteenth century. The wealth they acquired gave the lawyers an important part in the development of their towns and counties. The Wilshere family of Hitchin invested heavily in the grain and malt trade of north Hertfordshire. They acted as lawyers for Samuel Whitbread, the London brewer whose home was at Southill, in Bedfordshire, and in 1815 William Wilshere Jr became a partner in the brewery.

The same William Wilshere also turned his interests towards banking. In doing so, he joined large numbers of other country lawyers making the same type of investment. The first bank in Kendal, established in 1788, included one of the town's attorneys among its partners. The same was true of the banking partnerships at Newbury and Luton. Successful businessmen were also likely to invest in banking. This often came as a logical extension of the fact that they were acting as financial agents for their customers and creditors, arranging payments through London bankers on their behalf. Brewers were amongst those who invested in banking, their businesses often being some of the biggest in the late eighteenth-century market town. The two partners of the lawyer in Newbury's bank were both from one of the town's brewing families. W.B. Simonds, the founder of what was to become Reading's main brewery, added banking to his interests in 1790. The bank at Biggleswade was founded by a brewer in 1812. Other investors in banking included Philip Box, a draper, who established a bank at Buckingham in 1786, and Bedford's bank was founded by a coal merchant, Joseph Barnard, in 1799.

The bankers established themselves with the custom of the land-owners, the larger farmers and businesses and members of the professional classes. But theirs was a precarious business. All the banks were private partnerships, and their dependence on the partners' funds for capital left them vulnerable to local and national business troubles. Luton's first bank had to close when the death of one partner left the survivor with insufficient capital. The first bank in Macclesfield lasted thirteen years before it failed in 1800. It was taken over by Dainty & Ryle, a firm of cotton and silk manufacturers, and traded until 1842 when both bank and cotton mill failed. The town's second bank fared little better. It was founded in 1802 and collapsed in 1816. The failure of a bank was disastrous for a market town. Panic was created when one of Reading's banks ceased trading in 1816, and the crowd was so great at the bankruptcy hearing at the Bear Inn that those wishing to leave had to climb out of the windows.

All was not gloom for country bankers and their customers. Hundreds of small banks failed, but the survivors grew into perfectly safe institutions. The bank founded by Philip Box at Buckingham survived the trials of depression years, such as 1816, as well as its own crisis in 1824 when the coach bringing money from London bankers was robbed by highwaymen. The Simonds bank at Reading continued in business throughout the century before being taken over by Barclays Bank. Joseph Ashby Gillett founded a bank at Banbury in 1822, which became locally important, with branches in other towns such as Woodstock, Witney, Oxford and Abingdon. Gillett's Bank was finally merged into Barclays in 1919.

As those two examples show, banking became concentrated in the hands of large businesses. Legislation in 1844 allowed joint stock companies to enter banking, and soon there were extensive regional groups with branches in country towns. The London and County Bank was among the first of these. It opened a branch at Buckingham in 1846, and by 1850 was represented in market towns throughout most of the Home Counties. During the later part of the nineteenth century, the expansion of joint stock banks took the form of absorbing the old partnership firms.

One of the services provided in the market town was the publication of information through its newspapers, which grew in strength and numbers during the nineteenth century. In the eighteenth century, papers were only published at the principal towns. In Lincolnshire, there had been newspapers at Lincoln, Boston and Stamford, where the *Stamford Mercury*, first published in 1712, established itself as the principal journal for the counties of Lincolnshire and Rutland, holding that position until 1914. At times of political excitement, such as the crisis over parliamentary reform in the 1830s, short-lived news-sheets swelled the number of papers available for a while. It was not, however, until the heavy stamp duty on newspapers was removed in 1855 that the country town press expanded.

Increasing literacy furthered that growth, encouraging the desire amongst country people to inform and be informed. As Richard Jefferies noted, 'the smallest village event must be chronicled, or someone will feel dissatisfied, and inquire why it was not put in the paper'. The market town's papers thus came to have an important place in country life, despite their unglamorous nature when set beside the new popular national press of the *Daily Mail* and *Comic Cuts*. They reported town and country events and their role as a medium of advertising grew. As more labourers were able to read, they sought work through the classified advertisements rather than the hiring fairs. The growth of the press brought another new occupation to the country town, that of newspaper reporter. By the end of the century, newspapers were published in almost all Lincolnshire's towns. In Berkshire, where only Reading, Windsor and Abingdon had newspapers in 1830, all but Hungerford, Wokingham and Lambourn, of the county's ten towns had their own press by 1895.

=3=
Industries and Trades

'The old country town, with its ancient castle and quiet sombre-looking streets, cannot in the nineteenth century be classed amongst the busy and bustling scenes of manufacturing industry'. That was a description of Lancaster in the late 1840s, and, true enough, the market town was not on the whole the place to find the huge mills and factories belching smoke liberally across the neighbourhood. Yet, before the industrial revolution, market towns had been the manufacturing centres of the country. The industrial revolution changed the nature of manufacturing, turning workshops into factories, and took it to new centres. Some of these were market towns, which grew into industrial towns. The effect on other market towns, though, was the stagnation or decline of established industries.

Until the middle of the nineteenth century, the market town's trades and industries nearly all had their foundations in the surrounding countryside. Some were based on processing the produce of agriculture, whether grinding the grain, tanning the leather or dyeing and weaving the wool. Other local raw materials were processed in and around the town, such as wood for furniture and clay for brickmaking. The most successful industries generally outgrew their origins and brought in raw materials from far beyond the immediate countryside. The extensive cattle trade of Northamptonshire and Leicestershire provided the leather for the shoemakers in the towns of those counties, but as the industry expanded other sources of supply were tapped.

The second base upon which the trades and industries of the town were founded was to supply the needs of local people. The farming population formed an important market for blacksmiths, wheelwrights, harness makers and the makers of rakes, ploughs and other tools. All were to be found in the market towns, more so indeed, than in the villages where they might be expected to have gone to be even closer to their markets. There are two reasons for this. One is that a

Tanning, one of the long-established industries of the market
town. An illustration from an encyclopaedia published
in the 1850s.

The employees of Humphries & Sons are gathered in the main workshop for this photograph of 1910. This former market town wheelwright's shop had grown into quite a large wagon and carriage building business.

tradesman in a village could count on business coming only from his own and two or three neighbouring villages. A workshop in the market town had within a five mile radius fifteen or twenty villages, from which the farmers and landowners were likely to come to town at least every market-day. Besides those, there were the butchers, the bakers, the carriers and others of the town itself, who at times probably constituted the larger part of the craftsman's market.

The second attraction of the market town was that it usually had better communications than the village, enabling raw materials and fuel which had to be brought in to be acquired more cheaply and easily. Again, the most successful firms expanded away from the confines of their immediate markets. Iron foundries, established to make ploughs for local farmers, came to be selling steam-engines to all quarters of the country, and later to as far away as Australia.

Even the building trades were sometimes affected. Usually builders, carpenters, plumbers and similar trades were small businesses working in and around the town itself, but a few gained large contracts and expanded. The largest employer in Sleaford in the mid-nineteenth century was Kirk and Parry, builders' merchants and contractors. They employed 579 men in 1871, an eminence achieved by securing contracts for railway construction. In the 1860s they had been laying a new branch line from the nearby village of Honington to Lincoln, but most of their work was away from Sleaford, building stations at Leeds, Luton and Hertford, and engine sheds at King's Cross in London.

The limitations of transport before the industrial revolution meant that market towns were relatively self-sufficient. They all contained a wide range of craftsmen and manufacturers serving local demand. There were basket-makers and wheelwrights, rope-makers, curriers and tanners, coachbuilders, tinsmiths and others, in greater or lesser numbers from town to town. In the middle of the nineteenth century, improvements in transport, especially the railways, broke down the isolation which had sheltered the country tradesmen so that, although most of these crafts were still to be found in 1914, they were less ubiquitous. The miller who had once produced flour for the bakers of his town was forced out of business as his customers had their flour delivered from Bristol or Hull. George Sturt found customers deserting his wheelwright's shop at Farnham to buy 'steam wheels' from London, and light vans and carts made in factories in Bristol and workshops in Wiltshire.

Allied with improved transport, and having similar effects on the range of trades in the market town, were mechanisation and the larger size of manufacturing industries. Industry in the market town until the 1850s was on a small scale and was hardly mechanised. Business was based mainly in craft workshops where the distinction between manufacturing and retailing was so fine as to be meaningless. A wheelwright, for example, spent at least as much of his time repairing wagons as making them, and he might also sell the products of other manufacturers. He employed few men and less machinery; his tools were the bow saw, the auger and the spokeshave; no powered planes or electric drills.

The wheelwrights, shoemakers, watchmakers and other craftsmen were almost invariably one-man businesses. Numbers of employees other than the proprietor's family were small, often no more than one or two assistants or apprentices. The majority of businesses were on this scale into the middle of the nineteenth century. Daniel Taylor, a carpenter of Newbury in 1851, was a little exceptional in employing as many as four men and an apprentice, as well as having his son in the firm. Alfred Punn, who significantly perhaps described himself as a shoe manufacturer rather than a shoemaker, had three employees, and other craftsmen, such as printers and jewellers, sometimes had two or three men working for them.

The more industrial enterprises were rarely larger than the craft workshops. A windmill or watermill only needed one or two people to work it, and even steam-power did not make an enormous difference in the 1850s. The largest milling business at Colchester at that time employed only eight people. Malt-houses then were rarely of a size that needed more than two people in attendance. Breweries too were small, the largest in Colchester had six employees, while the biggest brickyards in that town employed seven men.

Amongst old-established industries, the one that employed large numbers was textiles. By the 1840s there were eleven mills in Norwich employing a total of 1,400. The largest silk mill in Colchester at that time had more than 400 workers, most of them women. Even in this industry though, the large mills were relatively recent, built as mechanisation was adopted. Before that, though the total numbers employed in textile manufacture were large, the handloom weavers were as often as not working in small workshops or at home.

Domestic outwork was common in the textile industry into the nineteenth century, and continued to be so until 1914 in other industries. Glovers at Witney and Woodstock in Oxfordshire employed countless women in the surrounding villages to make up gloves for them. Bridport had a trade in making sailcloth, twine and nets, based originally on locally grown flax, but by the second half of the nineteenth century using materials imported from the Baltic. A large part of the work of making nets was taken out to people in the villages. Indeed, individual villages had their own specialisations in this business, concentrating almost entirely on particular types of net.

In Bedfordshire and Hertfordshire, the plaiting of straw for hats was a large source of domestic employment for women in town and village alike. It was so important that young girls were sent to plaiting schools run by some of the older women in their back parlours. Anything else that was learned here besides the skills of plaiting was purely incidental, confined mainly to such necessities as being able to count the money handed over by the merchants in payment for their work. Since they gave no teaching in the three Rs, plaiting schools found themselves outside the law when elementary education was made compulsory in 1875, and after one or two successful prosecutions they quickly disappeared.

The principal towns in the plaiting district – Hitchin, Luton and Dunstable – each had large plait markets, to which the women brought their work, selling it to dealers who acted on behalf of straw hat makers in Luton, Dunstable, St Albans and London. There were smaller markets held in some of the other local towns, such as Shefford, Hemel Hempstead and Tring. All the markets took place in the open street or the market-place until the 1860s and 1870s when covered halls were built. But they came too late. Plait was being imported cheaply from China, and within a few years the trade had all but died in Hertfordshire and Bedfordshire. The plait halls closed; Luton's became the covered hall for the general market, while Hitchin's found an entirely different role as a mission church.

The clothing trades did not disappear. In Colchester in 1851 there were 532 women and girls employed as outworkers for the clothing firms there. This industry expanded in the following decades, supplying ready-made clothes for the shops of London. Although Colchester's firms opened factories using the latest industrial sewing machines – Hammond & Co. alone had about 1,000 factory workers in the 1890s – many companies, including Hammond & Co., continued to take clothes to outworkers in the town and villages to be sewn up. The only change made was that by 1914 deliveries were made by motor car instead of on horseback.

The industrial revolution brought greater mechanisation to industries that had traditionally been established in market towns. Workshops were replaced by factories, and businesses grew in size. This had conflicting effects on industry and the general economy of the towns. Some found that their traditional industries grew. Shoemaking, for instance, had been the principal trade in Northampton since at least the seventeenth century. From about 1815, the industry expanded rapidly in the town: in 1831 one-third of the men of Northampton were shoemakers, and by 1871 the proportion had risen to more than two-fifths. Mechanisation did not begin until the late 1850s, when machines for sewing the uppers were introduced, from then on the trade became increasingly based in factories. They were built in Northampton and in other towns of its county, such as

A market in progress in the new plait hall at Luton in 1878.

Kettering and Higham Ferrers. But while the development of shoe-making into a factory industry may have benefited Northampton, Kettering, Leicester and some other towns such as Norwich and Kendal, it was damaging to the craft trade elsewhere. The factories and the shoe shops, such as Stead & Simpson, who were amongst the first chain stores to reach market towns, undercut the craftsman shoemaker and took from him most of his customers at the lower end of the market. The small workshops had certainly not left the market towns by 1914, but their numbers were falling, and they were turning more to shoe repairs and retailing other firms' products.

Other industries followed a similar course. Small craftsman potters of the market towns suffered competition from the potteries of Stoke-on-Trent. The cabinet-makers found their livelihood threatened by factories in London making cheap furniture. Brick-making in a few areas grew into a major industry. The most prominent were brickyards around Peterborough where the Oxford clay lent itself to large-scale production. From a handful of small works in the early 1860s, brickmaking rose to become the second largest industry in Peterborough by the 1890s, with more than 1,000 employees. The railways were vital to the success of this industry, enabling the bricks to be sold throughout the country. The same combination of clay and rail transport enabled a large brickmaking industry to develop around Bedford. By the late nineteenth century, red bricks from Peterborough and blue bricks from industrial Staffordshire were beginning to compete with the local products of the market town.

TEXTILE INDUSTRIES

Perhaps the most important of the established industries of market towns to suffer competition from new industrial centres was the textile industry of southern England. Woollen cloth had been produced throughout the southern counties and East Anglia since the Middle Ages, when large-scale sheep farming had been widely established. The second foundation for the industry was flax, which was grown in many parts of lowland England. Upon this was based the manufacture of linen cloth, the knitting of stockings and other goods. The rise of the cotton industry in Lancashire and competition from new steam-powered woollen mills in the West Riding, especially from the 1780s as mechanisation was applied to the textile business, led to the almost complete collapse of the trade in the south.

The textile industry was already declining by 1750 in some parts of the south. Newbury had a large and famous trade in woollen cloth until the middle of the seventeenth century, when decline set in. Part of the old industry continued through the eighteenth century, principally in the manufacture of shalloon. In the early nineteenth century, John Coxeter's Greenham mills, which used the latest weaving machinery powered by water, provided employment for 100 people. Attempts to revive the industry on a larger scale proved unsuccessful, however. The pattern was repeated in a number of neighbouring towns in Berkshire and Hampshire, with some fragment of the old industry surviving in each; Andover, like Newbury, retained a sizeable trade in weaving shalloon. At Basingstoke, there

The tent-making room of a sack manufacturer's at Ipswich.
The photograph was taken about 1920, but hand work still
predominates in this part of the business.

was some small-scale manufacture of horse cloths and blankets in the
1750s.

Reading had entirely lost its woollen industry by 1750, but what
did survive into the nineteenth century was the weaving of flax into
sailcloth. Contracts to supply the Royal Navy were the mainstay of
at least one of the principal firms. Reading also retained some silk
weaving. In the first decade of the nineteenth century there were
about 500 people employed in workshops or at home making silk
handkerchiefs. Sailcloth, sacking, biscuit bagging and similar products were made in several other towns. At Abingdon there were
about thirty businesses engaged in this trade in the 1790s, which
'constituted the chief employment of the lower orders' of the town.
Sack-making continued to be Abingdon's biggest industry into the
1830s, but ten years later the trade was declining, and by 1867 only
two manufacturers were left in the town. The same happened to the
silk business at Reading. A factory was built in 1841, but closed
within a year or so, and in a few years the industry had completely left
the town.

In East Anglia, the textile industry was still active in 1750, though it was entering upon a rapid decline as cheaper cottons captured the markets. There were still said to be about 1,000 handlooms at work in Norwich in 1800, but decline had set in elsewhere by then. The clothworkers' guild at Colchester, the main centre of the trade in Essex, was wound up in 1800. The whole economy of several towns collapsed as the woollen industry declined. The market at East Bergholt ceased trading when the wool and flannel industry left the town. Dozens of other markets were also losing trade or had closed altogether by about 1800, and one major common factor was the disappearance of the clothing trade. The decline of this industry affected the outward appearance of the towns. Sudbury was once the local capital for the textile industry, but for some years after the trade moved away it 'possessed few attractions, and the houses belonged principally to decayed manufacturers'.

Much the same could be said of the textile industry in the south-western counties. It was initially somewhat stronger here, especially in Wiltshire and Gloucestershire where there was a tradition of high quality in the dyeing and finishing of the cloth which the mills of the North were slow to match. Several mills were built and extended during the late eighteenth and early nineteenth centuries at such towns as Bradford-on-Avon, Trowbridge and Nailsworth. At first they used water-power, which made a favourable impression on visitors: Frome was 'Leeds without its coal and dirt', thought William Marshall. Steam-power came late to Frome's mills; in most places it was introduced in the 1830s and 1840s. But, by then, decline was already under way, given dramatic character by the failure of two of the largest firms in Bradford-on-Avon in 1825, which pulled the local bank under as well. The troubles of the woollen industry brought problems to the town. Unemployment was widespread. The *Cheltenham Free Press* in 1840 reported on the problems of unemployed stocking knitters in Tewkesbury, who received an allowance of no more than five shillings a week, which was less than an agricultural labourer would earn at that time. Unemployed men from the shag weaving trades in Banbury and Witney were sent round the villages to look for farm work, but their search was fruitless, and they were 'beginning to riot, had not the yeomanry come in'.

One of the most striking effects of the decline of the cloth industry in the west, was that it stunted the development of the market towns.

The new Abbey Mills at Bradford-on-Avon. One of the last textile mills built in the West Country, they were constructed in 1874 and powered by steam.

Bradford-on-Avon was amongst the worst affected. Its population, which had been growing steadily from 7,302 in 1801 to 10,563 in 1841, fell sharply to 8,959 in 1851, as former cloth workers moved away. The population continued to fall during the second half of the nineteenth century, and by its end the town was predominantly an agricultural service and market centre. At that time there were still two mills at work. A new industry of rubber manufacture had come to the town, but it was minute compared with the former glory of the woollen trade. The next largest firms in the town were the breweries.

Parts of the old industry continued throughout the nineteenth century. Some mills at Trowbridge survived by making cloth for billiards tables, riding jackets, guardsman's uniforms and other special purposes. Despite losing some of its biggest firms, Frome's main industry continued to be the manufacture of cloth. The blanket-making industry of Witney continued to expand until by 1895 the mills were employing 700-800 of the town's population of 5,300. The industry of East Anglia experienced some revival as silk weaving expanded and new factories were built in the 1820s and

75

1830s. It lifted Sudbury out of the doldrums, and by the early 1860s about 1,500 were employed in the silk factories of the town. That proved to be about the peak, for shortly after that competition from France began to undermine the trade. Various specialised cloths continued to be produced in East Anglia. Sudbury also had some business in making bunting for ships' flags. Crapes to satisfy the Victorian taste in mourning were the mainstay of factories at Norwich and Braintree, where the output from Courtauld's mills increased twelvefold between about 1830 and 1850.

In the north-west, market towns were affected quite differently. Here, the production of woollen cloths such as checks, ginghams and linsey was increasing through the eighteenth century. To this trade was added cotton manufacture, principally of calicoes and fustians. Carlisle was the chief town in the far north-west, but the industry also grew in neighbouring places. About ten firms set up factories in Wigton in the 1780s and 1790s, making up the cloth produced by handloom weavers in and around the town. The arrival of these firms had dramatic effects on the development of the town, whose population all but doubled in the first thirty years of the nineteenth century.

But growth ended almost as suddenly as it had begun. The textile trade began to move away from this district in the 1840s. The worst period came during the 'cotton famine' of the 1860s when supplies of cotton were cut off by the American Civil War. The mills were on short time, if working at all, causing great distress to the workers. Charity soup-kitchens were arranged at Wigton every year from 1860 to 1863. Carlisle recovered afterwards; it was by now a major railway junction with other growing industries. It even managed to regain some of its textile business. Kendal was saved by its shoe factory, but other towns were less fortunate. Wigton lost over a thousand of its population between 1841 and 1871. The mills and factories were concentrated now in Lancashire and north Cheshire, where old market towns had been taken over by industry, though some, such as Stockport and Preston, never entirely lost the character of a market centre.

GRAIN PROCESSING

The agricultural processing industries of the market towns were
subject to forces of change similar to those affecting the cloth and
textile trades. In 1750, almost every market town in the country
numbered one or two millers and maltsters amongst the tradesmen.
They were, quite often, some of the more substantial businessmen of
the town. The specialised buildings they needed represented quite a
high capital investment and, since they were producing basic foods
for which there was a steady demand, their profits could be quite
high. They might invest these in other businesses, so that it was not
unusual to find millers and maltsters who were also corn dealers or
coal-merchants. Less usual was Peter Stubs at Warrington, who
made metal files as well as malt.

Peter Stubs gave up malting to concentrate on his file-making
business not long after the nineteenth century began. It was a move
indicative of the changes that were taking place in the grain processing trades, for, whereas in 1823 there were eleven maltsters in
Warrington, by 1900 there were none. The change hardly made any
difference to Warrington's economy, which was now based upon a
variety of metal and chemical industries. But for other towns, such as
Burford, which had once been noted as a centre for malting, the loss
of the trade was a greater set-back. Only one local brewer was still
making malt at Burford after 1900, and there was no flour mill in the
town. By 1914 there were numerous market towns where neither
flour nor malt was produced any more.

Improved transport took these trades to the towns most advan-
tageously placed for production. In the case of malting, that meant
the south and east of England where the best barley was grown.
Eastern England always did have a larger trade in malt, using the
barley grown in East Anglia, than other parts of the country.
Ware was the capital of the industry until at least the middle of the
nineteenth century. The maltsters of this town had established
themselves as the principal suppliers to large breweries in London,
and by the early nineteenth century their trade dominated the town.
There were about 20 maltsters working perhaps as many as 80 malt-
houses in this town with a population of 4,000 in the 1820s. Those
who were not directly involved in the maltings had an interest in the

trade. They were the malt and barley dealers, bargemen taking the malt to London, coal-merchants supplying fuel for the kilns and bankers financing the trade. Nearly all the small craftsmen and shopkeepers will have taken a keen interest in the movements of the barley and malt markets, since their prosperity depended on a successful malting business too.

There were more maltsters at Ware than at any other town, but the trade was also important over a wide area of north Hertfordshire. Such towns as Bishops Stortford, Baldock, Royston and Hitchin were all involved in producing malt for the London market. Further into East Anglia there were large numbers of maltsters at such towns as Beccles and Diss. River transport was influential in establishing the trade at the main centres. Its position on the Kennet was responsible for Newbury's having as many as thirteen maltsters in the 1830s, and in the early nineteenth century Newark's trade expanded with the aid of good transport provided by the River Trent.

The railways brought even more trade to the maltings of Newark. Both the number and size of the maltings increased during the second half of the nineteenth century. The maltsters of the town became prosperous and influential. Of the partners in one of Newark's leading businesses, Thomas Earp represented the town in Parliament between 1874 and 1885 and Sir William Gilstrap became a noted local benefactor, providing the money to establish a public library. Much the same happened at several market towns in the eastern counties, at Grantham for instance, or Ipswich and Bury St Edmunds. The railways provided the means by which the malt could be taken to the big breweries in London, Lancashire and Burton upon Trent.

The small malt-houses of the eighteenth and early nineteenth centuries, which needed only one man to do the work, were replaced by huge buildings, of four or five storeys occasionally. They could be notable features of the town: the brewers, Bass, for instance, built a set of eight malt-houses on the outskirts of Sleaford in 1902-6 on a prominent site alongside the railway line. The buildings had a frontage of 1,000 feet, longer than the average express train. But while these developments were taking place at towns in the east, further west towns were losing a trade which had served local needs for centuries.

Corn mills were found in and around almost all market towns in the eighteenth century meeting local demand, but, like malting, there

Inside a nineteenth-century malt-house. The illustration is of
a range of maltings built in 1884 at Shepton Mallet, typical
of the many built in market towns at this time.

were some notable concentrations in the south and east where millers
were producing for the huge markets of London or Liverpool. In
Defoe's time, there were several mills around Farnham and Guildford
grinding the corn sold at Farnham market. A good market for wheat
and river transport to take the flour to London were the foundations
for Newbury's milling industry. There were twelve millers in the
town in the 1830s, some with sizeable establishments. Shaw mills, for
example, had five pairs of stones, compared with the three usual in a
moderately-sized windmill or watermill.

Increased demand for flour as the nation's population grew
brought new mills to the country towns, especially from the 1820s to
the 1870s. In eastern England, some of these were windmills, and the
tall, brick tower mills were a characteristic sight in and around such
towns as Boston and Lincoln. From the 1830s, however, steam was
the dominant source of power for new mills in the market towns. In
Essex, a steam mill was built in 1848 at Chelmsford, and during the

next two decades others followed at such towns as Maldon, Romford and Halstead. As well as steam-power, the railway was an important factor in the operation of these mills. Nearly all were built close to the railway line to give ready access to the trains which took the flour away to customers in the cities.

The number of steam mills was small. Only six purpose-built mills were constructed in Hampshire by 1900, though there were many others where steam was added to an older watermill. They were not small mills though; when the Essex Steam Flour Mills at Chelmsford were destroyed by fire in 1860 the damage was estimated to be between £25,000 and £30,000. There were mills at Gloucester and Tewkesbury able to produce as many as 1,500 sacks of flour a week; the Shaw Mills at Newbury could produce 200 to 300 sacks a week. The size of the steam mills meant the displacement of older small mills. It was the millers in the villages who suffered most from such competition. When a new mill opened at Hitchin in the 1890s, windmills and watermills in villages nearby were quickly put out of business. The number of independent millers in the towns also declined: in the ten largest towns of Lincolnshire there were only half as many millers in 1913 as there had been in 1861. The small millers with windmills and watermills could not compete with the steam mills, and even less with the huge mills being built at Hull, Bristol and other major ports. The proprietors of the steam mills expanded into moderately-sized businesses. T.D. Ridley & Sons of Chelmsford were described as the 'largest buyers of corn in the Essex markets' at the time their steam mill burnt down in the 1860s. Their neighbours, William & Henry Marriage, had four mills around Chelmsford by 1906.

FOOD AND DRINK

In 1750 there were not many brewers in the market towns; that is, brewers in the modern sense of people who supply beer on wholesale terms to public houses, whether tied or free. In the eighteenth century the beer was brewed by the innkeepers who sold it, and there was no shortage of those in any market town. Brewing was, therefore, similar to most of the craft and retail trades, in being carried out on a small scale by producers who sold directly to the consumers. Whole-

Coxe's Mill, Weybridge, Surrey. A modernised watermill in the late nineteenth century.

sale (or common) brewers were at this time based mainly in London and other large towns, although there were some in the country districts. Burton upon Trent was beginning its growth from a small market town into a brewing metropolis. Its ale had been obtainable in London in the seventeenth century, and a number of breweries were founded between 1700 and 1750, among the famous names was Worthington in 1744. Burton's growth was hampered, however, by poor navigation on the Trent, and it was not until canals were built in the 1770s that brewing in the town really began to develop. Other towns better served by river navigations had common brewers in the early eighteenth century. Nottingham, Kingston upon Thames and Windsor were well known for the quality of their ales. Henley-on-Thames had two brewers in the 1720s.

The number of brewers in most market towns was small. In 1796, there were just two brewers in Newbury, one of Berkshire's largest towns with good transport, compared with thirty-five victuallers. The size of the breweries was also small; Robert Brakspear at Henley was brewing about 6,000 barrels a year at this time. Some of his contemporaries in towns not far away were producing more: John

May at Basingstoke brewed 8,000 barrels and J. & R. Ramsbottom at Windsor between 10,000 and 15,000 barrels. In London, Whitbread produced 137,000 barrels in 1800.

Brewers began to grow rapidly in number during the second half of the eighteenth century. Two carriers and coach proprietors, Backhouse and Hartley, started a brewery in Tadcaster in 1758 to serve some of the coaching inns. William Simonds, who had set up as a maltster at Reading a few years previously, added brewing to his business in 1768. In 1779 Messers Ind and Grosvenor bought the Star Inn at Romford where they concentrated on developing the thriving trade in supplying beer to other public houses in the town. By the 1830s the number of brewers had grown in all but the smallest towns – Newbury now had six – and their share of the market was growing steadily.

Further expansion came during the following decades, especially as railways enabled brewers to distribute their products over a wider area. For some towns brewing became an important industry. At Burton upon Trent it almost completely took the town over as the major firms grew into the biggest brewers in the country. At Northampton, Phipps & Co. and the Northampton Brewery Company became large concerns distributing their beer over a wide range of the south Midlands. The brewery founded by William Simonds at Reading was one of the largest businesses in the town by 1900. It had more than 200 employees and the firm's trade covered a large part of Berkshire and Hampshire. It had valuable contracts to supply the army at Aldershot and had built up an export trade to Malta and Gibraltar. Brewing was the main industry of Shepton Mallet by the 1880s where the Anglo-Bavarian Brewery Company was filling part of the gap left by the demise of the town's cloth industry.

As firms like the Northampton Brewery Company and H. & G. Simonds expanded, the number of independent businesses declined. This was especially true after about 1880, when consumption of beer fell and companies could only increase their trade by taking over another firm. So, after reaching a total of nine firms in the 1860s, the number of brewers in Newbury had dropped to seven in 1895. Grantham, which had five brewers in the 1850s, by 1896 had one, although it was a sizeable firm. There were also distribution depots for a number of brewers from outside the town, including two from Newark and Ind Coope from Burton. By 1914, brewing was rapidly

The yard of Lucas's Brewery at Hitchin in 1876.

disappearing from small towns – Kimbolton in Huntingdonshire or Thrapston in Northamptonshire, for example – while the advance of the major firms in Leeds and Tadcaster was taking the industry from major market towns in Yorkshire such as Driffield, Market Weighton and Skipton.

Food processing industries developed mainly from about 1875, becoming a new source of employment at market towns. There were some earlier food manufacturing trades. W. Mavor, in his report to the Board of Agriculture on Berkshire's farming in 1809, commented that Faringdon had a particularly good market for pigs, and went on to observe that 'no fewer than 4,000 hogs ... are killed and cured in this place annually; chiefly by two families, who have engrossed the greatest part of the business'. That might appear to be a large trade, and in early nineteenth-century terms it probably was, although it was well within the capacity of two or three family firms of pork butchers to handle those numbers of pigs as a sideline. That, in fact, was how the trade was organised, as Mavor tells us in his comments on Newbury, where there was a similar trade in curing bacon for sale to London. 'Any person', wrote Mavor, 'who can command from £20

83

to £50 sets up as a pig butcher, and sometimes increases his humble means to a decent capital'.

Two people who did precisely that, were brothers John and Henry Harris at Calne in Wiltshire in the early nineteenth century. One was a pork butcher and the other a grocer, and both entered the business of curing bacon. Their supply of pigs came mainly from the Irish ones that used to be driven from Bristol to London before the railways were built. Calne was one of the overnight stopping places for the droves. In the late 1850s, the two Harris businesses became factory-based when they introduced American methods of refrigeration to enable curing to be carried on through the summer, hitherto impossible. Twenty years later, the businesses each had about 60 to 70 employees and handled about 1,000 pigs every week. Finally in 1888 the two Harris firms, now passed on to the second generation, decided to combine their interests, giving them the largest bacon-curing business in England, employing 200, and drawing supplies of pigs from all over Wiltshire, Hampshire and the West Country, as well as Ireland.

Meanwhile, several other firms in Wiltshire joined in the bacon-curing business. Abraham Bowyer had opened a grocery shop in Trowbridge early in the nineteenth century. He left his successors two bacon factories, and in 1891 the business was converted into a public company. There were similar businesses of varying size at main towns in north Wiltshire, such as Trowbridge, Malmesbury, Westbury and Devizes. By the early twentieth century, these firms were producing other pork foods such as pies and sausages. Another major centre for pork foods was Melton Mowbray in Leicestershire. There were bacon-curers here, but the main speciality was pork pies. Five firms of pie-makers were based in the town in 1912, when they were said to be producing about twenty tons of pies each week. Meanwhile, the small bacon-curing businesses had not quite deserted such places as Faringdon and Newbury by 1914.

The trade in dairy produce was another old activity which began to grow into a factory-based industry at the end of the nineteenth century. Cheese and butter had always been made on the farms, and the trade to London and other large towns was handled by merchants in the market towns. The butter of Suffolk and Norfolk was esteemed in London in the eighteenth and early nineteenth centuries. Woodbridge was one of the main towns through which butter was

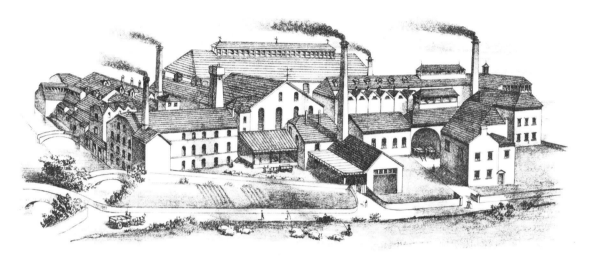

The bacon factory of Charles & Thomas Harris Ltd at Calne
in the 1880s.

shipped in Daniel Defoe's time, and into the 1820s Downham Market, in south-west Norfolk, had a busy market in butter which was sent to Cambridge to be forwarded to London. In Wiltshire, the trade was in cheese. There were six cheese factors at Marlborough in 1830, and the cheese markets here and at Chippenham, Devizes and Salisbury flourished throughout the nineteenth century. At Chippenham £5,000 was spent in 1900 on enlarging the cheese hall.

In 1873, the Anglo-Swiss Condensed Milk Company (now Nestlé) opened a factory at Chippenham to make condensed milk. Sixty-five people were employed at this factory, formerly a cloth mill, the earliest parts of it dating from 1802. By 1906, business had grown so that the number of employees had reached 163. The Anglo-Swiss Company had opened other factories at the same time in Aylesbury and Middlewich (Cheshire), adding a fourth at Staverton in Devon, in 1897 (this one in another old cloth mill). Other firms soon entered this business. In Wiltshire, a factory started making condensed milk and soft cheese in 1888, and in 1910 added skimmed milk powder and blancmange to its range of products. At Devizes a similar factory opened in 1889, this time producing mainly butter.

The silk factory which had been opened in Reading in 1841 and had closed shortly afterwards, received new occupants in 1846 when

Huntley & Palmer set up a biscuit bakery there. This factory laid the foundations of the modern fancy biscuit industry, changing it from a small-scale sideline of bakers and confectioners into a mechanised process. The types and even the names of biscuits, such as the Osborne, which are most widely eaten today in this country, were soon established by the new bakery. The partners also laid the foundations for much of Reading's future prosperity, for by 1914 their company was the largest in the town, with nearly 5,000 employees. Other businesses in the town had benefited, such as the Reading ironworks which supplied some of the firm's machinery. Flour millers in Reading and other towns of the Thames and Kennet valleys were kept in business supplying the biscuit factory. In Carlisle, one of Huntley & Palmer's main rivals had been founded in 1831 by J.D. Carr, and his firm likewise made a major contribution to the town's growth.

During the last quarter of the nineteenth century, new businesses began to grow in the market towns making prepared and packaged foods for the emerging mass market. There were jam-makers in Pershore preserving the fruit of the Vale of Evesham. There were other, mainly small, firms scattered about the country, such as the Ely Fruit Preserving Company, and Spring & Co. of Brigg who made lemon curd. Packeting dried peas was by 1905 one of the main sources of employment in Boston, and in 1913 another Boston firm began the canning of vegetables. Ketchups, pickles and sauces were also amongst the products of these small firms.

Sauces had a longer history as a product of market town industry. They had become popular as an item in upper-class diet in the late eighteenth century, and there were small firms in country towns who catered for this demand. Charles Cocks & Co. of Reading was one. Founded as a high-class fishmonger in the 1780s, the firm built up a trade in sauces extending to Bristol and into the Midlands. Lea & Perrin's Worcester sauce, introduced in 1837, was one of the first of these foods to be aimed at a wider market, and the firms of the later nineteenth century mostly followed that course. Their distribution of goods packed in bottles, tins and cartons stimulated the business of other firms in the market towns, such as the printers of labels. One firm which grew out of this demand was Rose Brothers of Gainsborough. It was founded in 1885 by William Rose, a barber who had invented a machine to wrap up tobacco, one of the items his shop sold as a sideline. From this, he built up a business making machinery for wrapping chocolate bars, washing blue, starch and other things, and the firm became one of the larger businesses in Gainsborough.

ENGINEERING

At the census of 1851 there were 62 men in Lincoln recorded as being employed in iron manufacture. Twenty years later, that number had reached 2,500, and by 1901 there were more than 5,000 men employed in what had become Lincoln's biggest industry. These figures give the barest indication of the remarkable rise of an engineering industry in this city. There were some large firms with national, even international reputations amongst Lincoln's engineers. The biggest was Clayton & Shuttleworth, who in 1871 employed 1,100. There were also small firms, such as the plough-makers John Cooke.

One of the foundations of the engineering industry in the market towns had been improvements in the techniques of iron founding made during the late eighteenth century, which reduced the cost and increased the durability of cast iron. By the 1850s, iron foundries were becoming common amongst the businesses of the market town. Most were producing goods to meet local demand for such items as ploughshares and kitchen ranges, as well as structural ironwork – pillars, railings and pipes. They were also responsible for many of the works associated with the town's improvement, such as mains gas pipes, lampposts and manhole covers. The foundry at Barnstaple, established by Thomas Willshire in the 1830s, was just such a firm. Although its business expanded to cover sub-contract work for firms in other parts of the country and for export, the basis of its trade was the supply of ironwork to the builders and implements to the farmers, brewers and other trades of north Devon. At the golden jubilee of the company there were about fifty employees.

The second foundation for the engineering industry of the market towns was the demand from farmers for new and more efficient implements and machines, from ploughs and harrows to threshing-machines and steam-engines. It was on this basis that some firms were able to grow from small workshops into large engineering enterprises employing hundreds of men. The farmers' demand grew especially from about 1835, and it is from this time that most of the large engineering firms of the market towns began to expand. Railways played their part too; in their growth from small foundries supplying a local demand into national and international businesses, the engineers relied on transport by rail. Few of the most successful firms were at towns without good railway connections. There were a few rule-proving exceptions. James Smyth & Son was one of the country's leading manufacturers of seed drills. Their base was at Peasenhall in Suffolk, about four miles from a railway station. R. & J. Reeves at Bratton, in Wiltshire, was another nationally known firm, at a similarly inconvenient distance from a railway at Westbury.

The importance of their local markets to the agricultural engineers is clear from the fact that almost all the large firms were established in towns in the south and east of England, where there were arable farmers requiring seed drills and threshing-machines. One of the earliest firms was Robert Ransome, later to become Ransomes, Sims & Jefferies. After a few years at Norwich, Ransome set up his foundry at Ipswich in the 1780s, where the port made deliveries of iron and fuel easier. Ransome made his name with the invention of self-sharpening ploughshares and with the development of patent interchangeable parts for ploughs, which enabled him to introduce some standardisation into his methods of manufacturing. His business grew rapidly, and even in the 1780s he was selling ploughs over a wide area of Norfolk and Suffolk. He sold through agents, who were nearly always shopkeepers and innkeepers in the villages and market towns.

Few firms grew so rapidly as early as Ransomes, who, by 1851, had 900 employees. Hornsbys at Grantham and Clayton & Shuttleworth at Lincoln were the next largest agricultural engineers at that time, employing about 400 each. The 1850s and 1860s saw rapid growth for the major firms as farming entered a period of prosperity and the railways opened up a national market. The Great Exhibition also helped. Clayton & Shuttleworth's manufacture of portable steam-engines was 209 in 1851, compared with 126 made in the previous eight years of the firm's existence, the additional orders coming mainly as a result of the Great Exhibition. By 1861 Claytons were producing 15 steam engines each week.

The successful agricultural engineers became the dominant industries of the market towns where they were based. They were usually the largest employers. Marshalls at Gainsborough, with a workforce

Some of the staff of the Reading Iron Works with an 8 hp
portable steam engine which had been exhibited at the Royal
Show in 1872, winning high praise.

reaching 1,500 by 1885 and 3,600 in 1904, were the mainstay of the
town's economy, which otherwise might have stagnated as its river-
side port declined. The factories established by these firms grew to
enormous size, a matter of some pride to the companies, who liked to
have panoramic views of the works on the covers of their trade
catalogues. Ransomes' works at Ipswich were spread over 10 acres by
the 1880s; the Britannia Iron Works at Gainsborough covered 28
acres in 1904. The proprietors of the agricultural engineering firms
often became leading lights in the civic life of their towns. Of
Lincoln's engineers, both Nathaniel Clayton and Joseph Shuttleworth were members of the city council, with Clayton serving as
Mayor in 1856-7. Joseph Ruston also played his part on Lincoln's
council and was a Member of Parliament; he was a supporter of the
Congregational church in the town and of local charities, being
responsible for the opening of a new children's ward at the county
hospital.

The dependence of the market towns on firms with such a close
connection with farming as the agricultural engineers, gave rise to its
own problems. When the firm of Samuelsons at Banbury, one of the
leading manufacturers of harvesting machinery, had to put men on

short time in 1879, it sent a shudder through the whole of the town's economy. After a run of poor harvests and financial losses, orders from farmers declined. It was a problem faced by all agricultural engineers, as English farming remained depressed for the next two decades. Most managed to survive, however, and in doing so saved the fortunes of their home towns.

There were two means by which the engineers weathered the storm. The first was to sell more of their agricultural machines and steam-engines abroad. Exporting was no novelty to the engineers, the larger firms had entered overseas markets early in their existence. Clayton & Shuttleworth built up a good trade in steam-engines and threshing-machines in Austria-Hungary in the 1850s; business grew to such an extent that they opened a factory in Vienna. In the last quarter of the nineteenth century, however, exporting became the dominant part of the engineers' business. There were several years when more than ninety per cent of Ransomes' output of threshing-machines and steam-engines were sold overseas.

The other way in which the market towns' engineers survived was by diversifying away from their established manufacture of agricultural implements. Again, this was nothing new. Nearly all the firms had taken on a wide range of general foundry work. In 1819, another time when demand for farm implements was low, a contract for the supply of ironwork in the installation of a gas supply in Ipswich was valuable in sustaining Ransomes there. More important in the long term, was Ransomes' decision to make lawn-mowers, which they started in the 1830s. As the home market in farm machinery declined from the late 1870s, the manufacture of lawn-mowers increased in importance for Ransomes. Other firms followed similar paths. Steam engineers turned increasingly to the production of road locomotives and traction-engines for fairgrounds. Aveling & Porter of Rochester, for example, abandoned agricultural work in favour of making road-rollers. The Wantage Engineering Company, whose main product had been threshing-machines, took up the manufacture of a variety of food processing machines, such as grinding machines for sale to coffee plantations. The old firm of Plenty & Co. at Newbury gave up work in agricultural implements in favour of marine engines and boilers.

The success of the engineers' policy of diversification was such that not only did they survive the agricultural depression, but several of

The smithy in the agricultural engineering works of
James Howard & Son of Bedford. An illustration from
the firm's catalogues of the 1870s.

them expanded. James Paxman's ironworks at Colchester was a small
agricultural business in the middle of the nineteenth century making
milling machinery, threshing-machines and steam-engines. During
the 1880s and 1890s, Paxman turned to the manufacture of oil and gas
engines, electrical and refrigerating machinery. Business grew and by
1900 there were more than 600 employees. In the wake of one
successful company like Paxmans, other engineering firms followed.
F.W. Brackett founded a business making pumps in 1899, the
Colchester Lathe Company was established in 1907, and there were
others until by 1914 nearly 2,000 people were employed in a wide
range of general engineering. There were similar developments elsewhere. At Newark, a small industry manufacturing ironwork and
implements for malt-houses developed into general boiler-making
and engineering, with new firms coming to the town during the
1880s. In 1899 they were joined by Ransome & Co., manufacturers of
ball-bearings.

Not all the engineering enterprises were successful, however.
There were quite a few manufacturers in market towns who produced
motor cars for a few years until growing competition forced them to

91

leave the business to the larger firms in Coventry. Rose Brothers of Gainsborough was one of these, making about 150 cars between 1904 and 1912. The Pick Motor Co. of Stamford was successful enough to survive into the 1920s.

The growth of industry in the nineteenth century had profound effects on the market towns. To those well-served by railways, new industries brought sustained growth. The others, the majority of country towns, where few or no new industries had settled, found their established structure of trade under threat from stronger industries in other parts of the country. These towns were slowly becoming little more than regional shopping centres.

It was during the last quarter of the nineteenth century that industry made its greatest impact on the market towns. It was then that some of the new industries of the age came to country towns: electrical engineering, the manufacture of oil and gas engines, food processing, clothing, bicycle manufacture. There was no lack of enterprise in these towns, for often the new factories were established by local people. All the new industries offered greater prospects for the town's growth than the traditional industries. Even the big steam flour mills of W. & H. Marriage at Colchester or the maltings of Bass at Sleaford could employ only about 100 men, whereas a successful engineering concern would be taking on many times that number of workers.

The effect was all the greater because these industries came to the market towns at a time when agriculture was weak, placing strain on the traditional connections of the town with farming. The towns with successful new industries were by 1914 rapidly drawing away from their countryside. For a few, like Peterborough with nearly 31,000 inhabitants in 1901 employed principally by railway companies and brickyards, or Colchester with a population of 38,000, it was becoming debatable whether they could still be called market towns at all. The interest formerly taken by the town's inhabitants in the prospects for the harvest was being replaced by concern for the progress of industry. Yet the break was far from complete. Peterborough was still a major corn market, strong enough to attract new maltings to the town in the 1890s. One of the town's great annual attractions was its agricultural show to which the railways brought people in their thousands from the east Midlands and East Anglia.

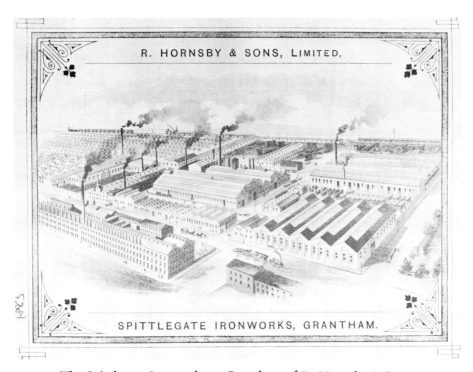

R. HORNSBY & SONS, LIMITED,

SPITTLEGATE IRONWORKS, GRANTHAM.

The Spittlegate Ironworks at Grantham of R. Hornsby & Sons.
By 1906 the works spread over 40 acres. This illustration
was printed in the company's catalogues of the 1880s when it
was not far short of that extent.

Carlisle was another town which had grown to a little short of 50,000 population by 1911. The people here worked on the railways, at Carr's biscuit bakery, at Cowans Sheldons' engineering works making cranes for railways and heavy industry, or in the printing works, brass foundries and other industries which had grown up. Yet Carlisle was still the major market for a wide area of northern Cumberland and south-west Scotland to which the farmers trekked week after week with their cattle and sheep. Banks, shops and commercial life generally continued to derive a lot of their business from the agricultural world, so much so that *Kelly's Directory* was still describing Carlisle as an agricultural town with industry attached to it.

=4=
Transport

Good transport was essential for the prosperity of a market town. Without it the town must surely decay, for the goods and people would pass by to markets elsewhere; with it, much could be made of little. Faringdon in Berkshire was situated at the meeting place of main roads running from Wiltshire to Oxford, and from Gloucester south-east towards Reading and London. This position was the town's main asset, for, as the trade directory for 1823 noted, 'the continual influx and reflux of travellers, with its extensive corn market and cattle fairs, combine in promoting its prosperity in the absence of manufacturing establishments'. Far greater benefits could accrue from good transport. Kendal owed the expansion of its textile industries in the eighteenth century in no small way to its place on one of the main routes from Scotland to the south, the modern A6. The provision of transport underwent rapid develment during the eighteenth and nineteenth centuries, as roads were improved, canals were dug and then railways were built. The effects on individual market towns could be great.

WATER

The best means of transport in 1750 was by water. Roads on the whole were in poor condition, making carriage by land slow and expensive. There was also the danger of highway robbery to be considered, a particular problem in some districts such as the Buckinghamshire Chilterns, where the woods provided convenient hiding-places. Carriage by water generally was cheaper and more convenient, since there were fewer hindrances and the boats could carry more than road wagons.

Coastal shipping together with navigable rivers were vital for the prosperity of many of England's market towns until the 1830s and

The wharves of Barnstaple. These were still used for some
shipments in the 1890s by one of the town's corn merchants,
whose wagons are seen in the background.

1840s when the main lines of railway were built. Water transport was
most important in the south and east of the country. More of the
long navigable rivers were in this zone enabling barges to reach far
inland to towns such as Nottingham on the Trent, Bedford on the
Great Ouse and Thetford on the Little Ouse. The River Yare was
navigable as far as Norwich, the Thames to Oxford and the Severn as
far as Shrewsbury. Besides these, there was a host of smaller rivers and
harbours around the coast of south-east England, all of which could
be used as channels for the trade of the countryside.

'The town of Colchester depends very much on its port', was the
verdict of one businessman there. Through it passed farm produce
bought by merchants in the town's markets to be sent forward to
London and the north-east. By far the greatest part of the traffic was
in grain: 22,000 quarters of wheat were shipped out of Colchester in
1836 as well as substantial quantities of barley, peas and beans. A large
part of the trade was in processed grain. Shipments for 1836 included
more than 113,000 cwt of flour and meal and 33,000 quarters of malt.

The port district of Colchester, the Hythe, consequently had a concentration of granaries, mills and maltings in and around the wharves. They were interspersed with timber-yards, more than thirty coal-yards and warehouses, for a large part of the incoming trade was of coal, timber, bricks and other building materials, as well as general groceries.

What was true of Colchester was also true of dozens of other towns around the east and south coasts. Some were larger ports. Yarmouth, the largest East Anglian port, had grain shipments three times as great as those of Colchester. Most, however, were smaller. Only 287 cwt of flour left Southwold in 1836, for instance, though barley shipments were nearly equal to Colchester's. Common to all ports though, was the content of the trade; agricultural produce went out, coal, timber and general merchandise came in. The outward trade was predominantly grain, though in Kent, for instance, wool was also an important item of trade from Faversham in the eighteenth century, and hops were shipped in great quantities from Maidstone, Faversham and Whitstable to London.

The coastal and inland trade produced employment for some of the townsmen in and around the wharves and on the boats. There were shipbuilding yards at several of the coastal towns. At Colchester, one was active well into the 1850s, despite the arrival of the railway to the town. There were as many as six boatbuilders listed in the Boston trade directory for 1856, while there were eighty-four shipowners and master mariners based in the town. The position was similar in inland towns where transport by river was especially important. There were two boatbuilders at Abingdon in the 1790s, and another at Reading. The trade continued at both places throughout the nineteenth century, but its nature changed from the construction of cargo barges to pleasure boats. One of Reading's boatbuilders advertised himself in the 1890s as a supplier of steam and electric launches, house boats and punts, adding that his clients included the Empress Eugenie and the Royal Military College at Sandhurst, neither of whom were likely to have been shipping flour to London.

Barge owners and barge masters were sometimes entered in the trade directories between the 1780s and 1830s, but their lists do not give a true picture because the operation of river and canal barges could be quite involved. Grain merchants, millers, maltsters and

Barges on the Thames at Abingdon in the early nineteenth century.

timber dealers often owned or had shares in the boats carrying their goods. Ownership could be spread more widely to bankers, solicitors, even some of the general craftsmen and traders of the town who might regard a small share in a barge as a worthwhile investment. The close connections between merchants and the carriers of their goods was especially notable at Ware, in Hertfordshire. The expansion of the malting trade here depended on the River Lea which enabled boatloads of malt to be sent the twenty-six miles to breweries in London. The barges returned with timber, coal and fertilisers for customers in rural Hertfordshire. It was an arrangement which proved strong enough to outlive competition from the railways, for grain was still being sent this way in the early twentieth century.

The importance of water transport was such that maintaining and improving the navigation was a major concern to traders of the market towns. This was certainly not new to the eighteenth century, but at that time investment in the improvement of waterways greatly increased. The River Lea to Ware was placed in the hands of new trustees in 1739, several of whom were prominent maltsters, corn factors and barge masters from the town. Work on the neighbouring Stort Navigation started in 1766, with strong support from the maltsters and bankers of Bishops Stortford. Improvements were carried out to most navigable rivers during the eighteenth century, sometimes involving extensive engineering work. The Kennet Navigation, undertaken between 1718 and 1721, was quite a major piece of work as eighteen locks were required along the eighteen miles of river from Newbury to Reading. The Navigation was a boon to Newbury, but its construction had aroused violent opposition from Reading, since goods formerly had to be transhipped there. The mayor of Reading even took gangs of his townsmen out to destroy the locks as they were being built.

Newbury proved to be a beneficiary of the building of the Kennet and Avon Canal, which was opened in 1810. The links made with Bristol and Bath meant that the general trade of the town greatly increased. Similar observations could be made of places such as Devizes in Wiltshire which now had better communications to the east. Canals in southern England helped the trade of other towns such as Cricklade or Basingstoke, but far less than the promoters had hoped. The Basingstoke Canal never paid its way, and in 1800 carried only about 18,000 tons of goods, well below the 30,000 tons a year forecast when the canal was promoted. No revival of old textile industries resulted at either Basingstoke or Cricklade, and the agricultural trade was not all that considerable. Indeed, the corn market at Cricklade was well on the wane by the 1840s, leaving incoming coal and groceries as the main traffic on the canal.

Canals had greater influence on towns in the Midlands and North, where old agricultural centres were brought into closer contact with the developing industrial and coal-mining regions. The Chesterfield Canal, opened in 1774, strengthened the east-west route from Lincolnshire to Derbyshire and south Yorkshire. The price of coal at Retford, along the route of the canal, dropped by a third as soon as it was opened, and both here and at neighbouring Worksop, industrial activity increased in the following years. The old-established processing trades of milling and malting both expanded; there were twice as many flour mills at Retford in 1832 as there had been in 1774. New industries also developed, such as paper-making at Retford, saw milling and furniture-making at Worksop. Textile mills were opened at both towns, though without lasting success; nearly all had gone by the 1820s.

The canals across the Pennines had similar effects on towns further north. Skipton had always been the main corn and cattle market for Wharfedale and trade grew when the Leeds and Liverpool Canal opened smoother communications to Burnley, Blackburn and other

Narrow boats of one of the town's grain merchants on the
Kennet and Avon Canal at Newbury in 1910.

Lancashire towns. Some cotton mills also came to the town, which,
unlike those at Worksop, remained as Skipton's largest employers
into the late nineteenth century.

ROADS

Even the towns with the best water transport still depended heavily
on roads. There were certain types of traffic that rarely went by water
– passengers was one of these, although there were some passenger
barge services, for instance on the River Witham from Boston to
Lincoln, continuing up the Fossdyke to Gainsborough. Quite a
network of sail, horse and steam packets covered this route in the
early nineteenth century. The steamboats, especially, were so popular that traffic began to be drawn away to Lincoln's markets at the
expense of Horncastle and Tattershall. But these were exceptions.
People usually travelled by road until railways were built. So, too, did
livestock; it was uncommon for animals to be sent either by coastal
ship or by barge. Perishable goods and goods of low bulk and high

value generally went by road, but so did other goods as occasion arose. Sometimes the river navigations were not kept in good repair, especially in the upper reaches, forcing goods on to the road. It was because the navigation of the Thames had become 'so much neglected, and so tedious', that bacon cured in Faringdon was sent by road to London.

In areas without navigable waterways, road transport was essential for all traffic, and the market towns were generally at the meeting points of major roads. Towns of regional importance in the north, such as Richmond, Settle and Skipton, were at junctions of north-south routes and the cross-Pennine roads. Further south, Barnsley had been established on the crossing of the main road south from Richmond to Huddersfield and the route from Wakefield to Sheffield. The roads linking these towns were remarkably direct, going straight up one hill and down the next. In the early eighteenth century, they were predominantly tracks passable only by pack-horses.

Difficult terrain was not the only problem facing road users in the early eighteenth century. The standard of road maintenance was poor. 'I remember the roads of Oxfordshire forty years ago', wrote Arthur Young in 1813, 'when they were in a condition formidable to the bones of all who travelled on wheels.' There is an abundance of similar complaints that roads were so ill-cared for, so full of mud, deep ruts and pot-holes as to be almost impassable. It was not only the open roads that were bad, the streets inside the towns were just as likely to be muddy and full of holes. Under conditions such as these, patience was needed in undertaking journeys by road. Letters sent post-haste could take as long as seven or eight hours to cover the twenty-four miles from Minehead to Taunton at the end of the eighteenth century. The Reverend Sydney Smith's progress was not much faster: 'It took me 9 hours to go from Taunton to Bath before the invention of rail roads. I suffered between 10,000 and 12,000 contusions before stone-breaking MacAdam was born'. The problems were worse in the winter, when travel became really slow, sometimes impossible, so full were the roads of mud and deep puddles. Indeed, it was because transport by road was so difficult during winter that the great general fairs were important. Many of them were held in late summer or autumn to give shopkeepers and householders a chance to stock up before winter's rains and snow blocked the roads.

The roads were improved during the eighteenth century as turn-pike trusts took over the responsibility for maintenance from the parish authorities in whose hands it had been since the sixteenth century. The trusts were able to be more effective as they had wider powers to raise capital through loans and to raise revenue by charging tolls on traffic. Those who subscribed the capital of turnpike trusts were predominantly the major landowners along the routes. They were generally wealthy, and they were interested in promoting the improvements of their estates, both the agricultural land and their holdings in the market towns. The nobility, gentry and farmers thus contributed £3,050 of the £4,000 raised by the Worksop-Attercliffe Trust. Individual subscriptions could be large. Lord Beauchamp contributed £1,500 of the £2,000 required by the Evesham-Alcester Trust in 1778, and the Duke of Norfolk lent £6,000 to the Sheffield-Glossop Trust.

As well as the landowners, there were numbers of the market town's merchants prepared to invest in the turnpikes. Investors in the Hitchin-Bedford Trust in 1757 included a tanner, four maltsters, a baker and two drapers. The number of tradesmen investing in the trusts was small, however. Although four innkeepers, a shopkeeper, a hatter and a horse dealer were included amongst the supporters of the Banbury-Barcheston Trust in 1804, forty-nine of the sixty-two sub-scribers were landowners or farmers. The contributions of the merchants were similarly small when set beside those of the land-owners, although there were exceptions: £350 out of the £1,300 subscribed to the Dunchurch-Southam Trust came from tradesmen.

The smallness of the provincial traders' investment in turnpikes was mainly due to the fact that they were on the whole less wealthy than the landowners. But in addition, they were not always convinced that turnpike roads would benefit them. It was the tolls that were their main concern. The inhabitants of Leighton Buzzard in 1810 petitioned the House of Commons against the Bill for the Aylesbury-Hockliffe Trust. The road was planned to pass through Leighton, and the prospect of paying tolls did not appeal to the people there. Earlier, in 1729, the coal-merchants of Bedford had complained about the payment of tolls, arguing that because they made so many journeys, the sums they would have to pay in tolls would adversely affect their trade. The corporation of the town, moreover, said that corn merchants were conducting their business in villages outside the town rather than pass through toll-gates.

Far more effective than tolls in harming a town's trade, though it did not provoke so many petitions to Parliament, was the fact that road improvements could alter main routes, diverting traffic away from some places. Tideswell, in the Peak District of Derbyshire, was one place that suffered, when the new turnpike road to Buxton was taken some way to the south of the town. Wirksworth, at the southern end of the Peak, was also isolated. The town was formerly at a crossing of north-south and east-west routes, but the opening in 1820 of a new road through the southern Derwent valley (the route of the modern A6 to Matlock) diverted traffic away to the east. Even a town like Skipton, an acknowledged local capital, found that not all the new roads were to its advantage. The town gained from its position on the main turnpike from Kendal to Keighley, an important link between wool producers and West Riding mills. But Skipton's traditional hold on the trade of upper Wharfedale was lost for a while when the owners of lead-mines around Grassington built a road not to Skipton, but to the smaller town of Pateley Bridge. Skipton's loss was not permanent, for the construction of the Leeds and Liverpool Canal brought the Wharfedale trade back, attracted by the supply of cheaper coal.

Towns served directly by the turnpikes could benefit considerably. Stow-on-the-Wold was one that did. Situated at the eastern end of the Cotswolds, far from navigable rivers, Stow was dependent on roads for its trade. The road from Evesham was placed under a turnpike trust in 1736, and in the following decades the other roads radiating from Stow were similarly improved, the last being the route to Tewkesbury in 1792. Stow now had better direct road links to London, the Midlands, Bristol and Gloucester. Long-distance traffic to and from these places increased, the demand for services in the town grew, and Stow's attractiveness as a local market and commercial centre was enhanced.

Long-distance road carriage services had been in existence since at least the sixteenth century, but the improvements made to roads in the eighteenth century greatly helped their development. By the end of the century, there was a complex network of services linking market towns with each other and with the major cities such as London and Bristol. There were carriers based in each town operating long-distance and local services. In the 1790s, Leader's stage-

Kendal and Ulverstone
COMMON CARRIER.

JOHN CLARKE,

of Haverthwaite, near Ulverstone,

BEGS LEAVE TO INFORM HIS FRIENDS AND THE PUBLICK IN GENERAL, THAT

HE HAS ESTABLISHED

a regular Conveyance for forwarding Goods betwixt

KENDAL AND ULVERSTONE,

BOOTLE, RAVENGLASS,

EGREMONT, WHITEHAVEN,

AND ALL THE INTERMEDIATE AND ADJACENT PLACES.

⁂ All Goods consigned to him, the Publick may depend will be delivered with the utmost Care and Dispatch.

Leaves the New Inn, *Kendal*, every Wednesday and Saturday at Noon, and arrives at *Haverthwaite* in the Evening ; and is at the Brown Cow Inn, *Ulverstone*, every Monday and Thursday Morning, and returns to *Haverthwaite* the same day.

J. C. hopes, by his due Attention to Business, to merit a Share of Publick Support.

October 7th, 1811.

[Soulby, Printer, Ulverston.]

A handbill advertising a carrier's service between Kendal and Ulverston in 1811.

wagon from Faringdon would leave the Bell Inn every Saturday and Tuesday for London, taking goods at *2s. 6d.* per cwt. Towns on main routes were served in addition by wagons coming from further afield. Hungerford, on the busy road to Bath, simply had 'many wagons'

103

passing through, but elsewhere the directories were usually more specific. About ten wagons each week stopped at Abingdon on their way to London from Gloucestershire. Chesterfield, Mansfield, Newark and Grantham were all stopping places for the wagon operated by Royle between Sheffield and London. The same carrier had another wagon going from Sheffield to London, this one serving Nottingham, Loughborough, Leicester, Market Harborough and Northampton on the way. Cross-country services followed a similar pattern.

Improved road services increased the speed and efficiency of road carriage. Roads were so bad in the early eighteenth century that pack-horses were still commonly used, not just over the Pennine tracks, but throughout much of lowland England. In the 1760s, there were said to be as many as 150 pack-horses setting out each week from Manchester to Bridgnorth and Bewdley, where goods could be transhipped to barges on the Severn. The building of turnpike roads soon transferred goods to wagons, which were more efficient carriers. Higher speeds and better construction of vehicles enabled some express goods services to be built up in the early nineteenth century, such as the light fly vans which carried fish overnight from Yarmouth to London.

The most striking effect of turnpike roads was that they paved the way for development of express coach services. Coaches could travel more quickly, and, as the standard of coachbuilding was also improving, travel was becoming more comfortable. New, high-speed services began to operate from the middle of the eighteenth century. They were often known as flying machines, and such apparently curious announcements as 'The Abingdon Machine began Flying on Monday the 5th of April' were not unusual in local newspapers of the day. The number of services increased rapidly from the 1780s. By 1830, towns on the major routes had dozens of coaches pass through each day: forty-four called at Marlborough, and in Bedfordshire, Dunstable was served by nearly fifty coaches running from London to Birmingham, Chester and Liverpool.

On routes served by more than one coach, there could be fierce competition between rivals, sometimes not merely involving the coachman. When James Eade started running a coach from Petworth to London in competition with Robinson's coach which called there on its way from Littlehampton the whole town was caught up in the

The High Street in High Wycombe in the 1770s. A coach is
emerging from the Red Lion, one of the principal inns of the town.

rivalry. Most of the Petworth townsmen took up Eade's cause, the
more heartily, most likely, because Lord Egremont at Petworth
House supported Robinson. 'Half the town of all classes used to
assemble to see the rival coaches come in', an old resident recalled of
this time. 'The passengers were hurrayed or hissed in turn'. While
garlanding the horses of their favourite, the crowd was likely to aim
rotten fruit at the rival coach. This episode was short-lived, as Eade
went out of business; but on other routes stiff competition, without
such dramatic features, continued.

For the people of the market towns, the coaches offered a valuable
link with the outside world. The tradesmen were able to widen
business contacts, by making a trip to Bristol or London. It was
necessary to be fairly determined to make use of some coaches,
though. The 'Monarch' on its journey from Bristol to London
probably picked up few people at Hungerford, as its call at the Stag's
Head there was at one o'clock in the morning. The return journey

was no better, reaching Hungerford at two o'clock in the morning. Fortunately for the inhabitants of Hungerford, there were nine other coaches running to London at more respectable hours.

The greatest effect of coaching, though, was in the increased demand for hotel services. It is clearly visible in almost every market town today, where there are inns which still show the signs of having been rebuilt and modernised some time between 1780 and 1830. Extra accommodation and better stabling was added, and quite often a smart brick facade was built in front of an older timber-framed building. Enlarging the George at Stamford cost more than £1,830 in the 1780s. New inns were also built, such as the George Hotel at Grantham in 1780 and the new Stamford Hotel in 1810-3. By 1826 the hotel trade was the largest source of employment in Grantham. The supply and provisioning of horses for the coaches was a considerable part of the inns' work. They kept a supply of post horses ready to change the coach teams. One of Newark's busiest inns, the Glentham Arms, kept as many as twenty-five pairs of horses. Besides the ostlers and stable-lads, a few inns, like the Angel at Wetherby and the George and Dragon at Banbury, had a shoeing smith on the staff.

The railways killed the coaching trade almost overnight. The Saturday after the railway was opened from Bedford to Bletchley, a junction with the line to London, the 'Bedford Times' coach made its last journey to London. The pattern was repeated across the country. Long-distance traffic quickly moved to the railways, and coaches stopped running on routes in direct competition with trains. They lingered a while longer where railways had not yet been built, or where they could provide cross-country and feeder services complementary to the railway. The damage to some market towns was considerable. Dunstable, on the main coaching road but only on a branch railway, stagnated for about thirty years, and Hungerford fared little better.

Although the railways quickly captured long-distance traffic, local journeys in and around the towns could keep country roads busy. Some coaches continued to run on short journeys between neighbouring towns. There was one running between Fairford and Cirencester in the 1890s, for example. Horse-drawn omnibus services were also developed, apparently in a rather haphazard way, depending on a local enterprise deciding it was worth operating a service. One such omnibus ran for several years from the mid-1870s between Lambourn

'The Trout' local coach to Cirencester outside the Bull Hotel at
Fairford in the 1880s. The importance of catering for
tourists is shown by the model bicycle added above
the hotel's signboard.

and Newbury. It ran on Monday, Thursday and Saturday, charging a
single fair of 1s. 6d. for the twelve-mile journey. The larger, expanding towns acquired regular local bus services between residential areas
and the town centre, and in a few places these were joined by
tramways. The Ipswich Tramway Company opened its first length of
line from the railway station to Cornhill in 1880. This steam-
operated system was soon extended to other parts of town. Lincoln
and Grimsby both had horse tramways, opened in 1883 and 1881, and
converted to electric traction early in the twentieth century.

Local transport services from the village to the market town were
provided by the carriers. Their services were quite independent of
any other part of the transport system. They were not feeders to
canals or railways, but provided market-day transport for people and
goods from the village to reach the town. The number of carrier
services increased through the nineteenth century, quite unaffected
by the railways since they were not competing with one another.
Reading, for instance, was served by 205 carriers' routes in 1867 and
238 by 1895; at Guildford the number of services increased from 106
in 1854 to 166 in 1914.

Carriers' services were predominantly local. Usually the carrier

A typical carrier's wagon. Not perhaps the height of comfort, but
it was cheap and better than walking.

himself was based in one of the villages he served, and the routes he
covered were seldom longer than fifteen miles, representing approxi-
mately the limit of what could comfortably be accomplished as an
out-and-home journey in a day. There were exceptions, and these
mainly came into the largest towns. Newcastle-upon-Tyne had
carriers coming from Alnwick and Bishop Auckland, thirty-four and
twenty-eight miles away respectively. A carrier from Diss made the
twenty-mile journey to Norwich, another ran a service from Cromer,
twenty-three miles. The services into Reading included one from
Farnham, twenty-five miles distant, and another from Alton, which
travelled well over thirty miles when detours to call at villages were
taken into account.

The number and range of the carriers' services were one of the
strongest indications of the status of a town and the strength of its
retail market and shops. For, while Reading had more than 200
carriers in 1895, Faringdon was served by only 11. The relative decline
in Faringdon's economy was marked by a decline in the number of
carriers: there had been 15 in 1867. Some of the services that did serve
Faringdon were not running on the town's market-day, but instead
were taking people from the town to larger markets at Oxford,
Abingdon or Cirencester.

Some carriers took only goods, some only people, but most carried

A view of High East Street, Dorchester, about 1900. Despite
the sign of Channon & Sons, this is still the age of the
horse-drawn carriage. The street, though well-paved and
drained, has the dustiness and muddiness of pre-motor roads.

both. Their passengers were villagers going into town for the markets
and shops. They needed patience, for the journey was leisurely. The
carrier's wagon would trundle round the village and call at farms on
the way to pick up parcels to take into town. There might be linen to
take to the steam laundry, a sack of flour for the baker, but mostly the
goods consisted of fruit, vegetables, eggs, butter, poultry and other
produce being sent to supply the shopkeepers and some of the
hoteliers of the town. Each call would take a few minutes, quite often
more if the carrier was detained for a cup of tea and a chat. A short
journey could thus take hours: as Arthur Randell recalls in *Sixty
Years a Fenman*, Mrs Blades' wagon from Magdalen would reach
King's Lynn, seven miles away, in about three hours. Not that it
mattered to the ten or so passengers, who spent the time catching up
on the week's gossip.

On arrival at the town, the carrier would deliver the various parcels
before stopping at an inn where both horse and driver found refreshment. The wagon was usually left out in the street, and with so many
carriers coming into town, the streets of a busy market town could be
quite crowded with their vehicles, to say nothing of the various carts
and gigs of farmers and traders visiting the market. The authorities at
Banbury tried to introduce some tidier arrangements for parking in

the middle of the nineteenth century, but were overwhelmed by the outcry they provoked. After dinner, the carrier went round the shops and market buying on behalf of people in the village unable to come themselves. There were many quarters of tea, pounds of sugar and pieces of meat to be bought, and an enormous variety of household items from needles, lamp oil and crockery to patent medicines and wallpaper. After three or four hours in the town, the wagon was loaded up and made the journey home. Carrier services flourished until the First World War. Some, like W.H. Giles, a carrier to Newbury from Hungerford and Kintbury in Berkshire, modernised their services with motor vans. After the war even that was not enough for them to withstand competition from the bus services which were extended into the villages.

RAILWAYS

Enough has been said in earlier chapters to indicate that railways had a marked effect on the fortunes of different market towns. To some the railways brought additional trade, to others they brought competition from stronger markets, and to all they brought the results of the industrial revolution. In part, the railways confirmed an existing trend whereby the larger towns grew at the expense of the smaller ones, but locally there were many exceptions. Everywhere, the ability of the railways to upset old traditions by introducing competition from the new industrial centres made their impact on the market towns greater than it was on the major cities.

The effect of the railways on market towns was the more remarkable in that it was often rather arbitrary, almost accidental. Some towns gained by the railway, others lost by it, not necessarily on their own merits, but on the attractions of larger centres. The first generation of railway companies were not attracted to country towns. They were interested in the established and rapidly growing industrial and commercial towns. They wanted to reach London, York, Birmingham or Manchester, and it did not matter too much whether or not they passed through Abingdon, Stamford or even Northampton. Chesterfield, one of the larger towns of north Derbyshire, had nothing to attract the railway builder of the 1830s. It was just another market town, according to the North Midland Railway's engineer, 'not of any great trade; there are markets'. The trains went through Chesterfield only because there was no other sensible way of going from Derby to Leeds. Abingdon was less fortunate. There were alternative routes for the Great Western Railway to follow. One of the landowners along the way that would have taken the line through the town began to be obstructive. The company was determined to reach Oxford and took the easy course to avoid trouble. The line was built three miles to the east of Abingdon, leaving out a county town with more than four thousand inhabitants who were generally in favour of having a railway.

Even the people of the market towns themselves could not always see the point of having railways in purely agricultural areas. When the Eastern Counties Railway was being projected in the 1830s, the company's promoters sought support in the principal towns of Essex, Suffolk and Norfolk; they found instead several tradesmen, aided by local newspaper editors, who spoke out against the railway. They argued that with perfectly good waterways, there was no need for a railway. This seems to have been the prevailing view amongst the businessmen of Colchester at this time. When the railway was actually built their interest in the line was mainly a desire to prevent its extension for fear trade might be diverted to rival towns. In particular, they opposed extension to Ipswich, where the port was a strong competitor with Colchester's, and made a devious counter proposal for a line from Colchester through Hadleigh to Bury St Edmunds, bypassing Ipswich. Needless to say the men of Colchester lost this battle, and when the new railway opened in 1846 with brass bands playing in Ipswich there was not a flicker of interest in Colchester.

Indifference and opposition to railways from country town businessmen was on the whole a minority opinion. Merchants and manufacturers in the 1830s and 1840s were likely to favour having a railway. A meeting in Norwich in 1836 to discuss the proposed Eastern Counties Railway voiced support. J. Harvey, an industrialist from Norwich, said he 'was personally acquainted with 20,000 people at Norwich and hardly knew anyone who was not favourable to a railway ...' Several other Norwich merchants spoke in favour of the railway. They urged their support principally on the grounds that a railway would take their goods away to London more quickly and at lower cost. Underneath such statements was their belief that the railway would increase their trade, often a hope that being on the rail network would suddenly bring cotton mills to their town, and always a fear that without a railway rival towns would gain their trade.

A combination of these hopes and fears prompted local action to construct branch lines to serve towns bypassed by the main routes. The London and Birmingham Railway's line passing well to the west of Bedford soon led local interest to promote a line from Bedford to Bletchley. The chairman of the company, T.J. Green, was a coal merchant, mayor of Bedford in 1843-4 and county treasurer. Among his directors was Robert Newland, a brewer in the town. The Harris family, bacon-curers of Calne, were instrumental in securing a branch to Chippenham on the Great Western main line in 1864. Faringdon gained its branch line in 1863, with leading members of the town responsible for its promotion.

The railways brought new business and employment to market towns. Their own contribution to employment was not a small one, for theirs was a business dependent on labour. The staff at Hitchin station, from stationmaster to errand boy, numbered about 70 early this century. To this number could be added the men working in the engine sheds. Hitchin was a busy junction, but even at smaller places there could be as many as 20 employed at the station. A number of railways had their engineering and repair workshops at country towns. Oswestry was the headquarters of the Cambrian Railways' locomotive department. Doncaster had been a modest town until 1853 when the Great Northern Railway's locomotive workshops opened there, employing 949 men. With wives and families, they increased the population by nearly 25 per cent. The Great Western Railway turned Swindon from a small town off the main routes into a busy place of 45,000 people by 1914. The Great Northern was also a major employer at Peterborough, with 800 workers in its engine sheds by 1865, but growth was furthered by independent wagon-repairing firms. Chippenham similarly gained from the arrival in 1910 of the Westinghouse company, makers of brake and signal equipment for the railways.

The movement of goods and passengers to and from the market towns was made easier by the railways. They gave opportunities for more people to travel. A stage-coach could take four passengers inside and up to twelve seated somewhat precariously on the roof. That meant that Dunstable with its fifty coaches a day could offer

The railway station at Brandon, Suffolk, shortly after it was opened in 1845. The railway hardly helped this small town to prosper; Brandon was now on a direct line to Ely and Norwich, the regional centres.

seats to no more than 800 passengers, and, of course, most of those were probably taken by people passing through the town. Even the short trains with small carriages in use on the early railways could easily exceed the capacity of the stage-coaches.

Far more important than the number of seats available, was the lower cost of travel. Coach fares could vary considerably depending on the amount of competition, which on some routes was fierce. The fare from Abingdon to London was 14s. in 1796, which was about 2¾d. a mile. The 'Norwich Telegraph' charged £1.6s. for the journey to London. To those fares had to be added the sixpences given in tips to coach drivers, guards and hotel staff along the way, which could make the total outlay some 25 per cent greater. Those fares were for inside passengers. Outside riders usually paid half, but for both classes the railways cut fares at first by about a third. Third-class passengers proved to be the biggest gainers, especially after a standard rate of a penny a mile was enforced on the railway companies by Parliament in 1844. During the second half of the nineteenth century, cheap excursion trains were being run to take the labouring people to some of the major holiday fairs such as Lincoln's April Fair or the

Nottingham Goose Fair, and then further afield to the seaside at Skegness, Blackpool or Bournemouth.

The railways increased the movement of people into and out of the towns, and, although there were places formerly on main coaching routes and now with at best a branch line where the inns and hotels lost trade, elsewhere hoteliers gained. Their trade might be slow to pick up at first, but as farmers, cattle dealers and corn merchants travelled further to markets, as commercial travellers made their rounds of the country town shopkeepers, and as more people took holidays in the country, so business grew. By the 1880s and 1890s the effect can be seen in any business directory where, even at the towns of moderate size, there was likely to be at least one astute hotelier advertising that he sent omnibuses to meet every train.

The movement of goods into and out of the market towns passed to the railways. The Eastern Counties Railway, one of the most rural of major companies, captured all but a fragment of the grain which had gone by barge and coastal vessel from the East Anglian towns to London, Liverpool and Newcastle. The incoming cargoes of coal, timber and salt were also transferred to the railway. The change was not as instantaneous as the annihilation of stage-coach services had been. It took a few years before competition from coastal and inland shippers was defeated. A writer in the *Norwich Mercury* declared that 1848 was the year when prosperity left the port of Yarmouth, for by then, two-thirds of the grain trade was carried by rail, and at most other places during the late 1840s and 1850s the railway won the lion's share of the traffic.

The success of the waterways and coastal shipping in holding off railway competition was partly the result of strong rearguard action by some leading merchants who believed that boats were best. Debate raged particularly fiercely in Colchester, and during 1846 and 1847 an unsuccessful attempt was made to have major improvements carried out to the docks and river channel. There were some possible advantages to the merchants in keeping the port busy, because while shipping remained an effective competitor with the railway, they were gaining from the price-cutting in rates of carriage. Even so, it is ironic that after all the arguments it was the railway which really brought prosperity to Colchester. By the 1890s scarcely any ships used the port.

Colchester was one of the fortunate towns, for the possession of a

The staff of Hitchin railway station, about 1906.

railway connection did not always lead to the rising prosperity which
the inhabitants of market towns often expected. Salisbury did not
become the 'Manchester of the South', as was confidently forecast at
the opening of its railway; nor did Bury St Edmunds experience the
hoped-for industrial and commercial boom. This town was not on
the main lines from London to Norwich or King's Lynn. It did, however, have a railway built in the 1840s from Ipswich to Newmarket.
But by the 1860s, the businessmen of Bury were disappointed that
trade and industry were not growing, in fact rather the reverse as
the railway drew trade away to Ipswich, Cambridge and Wisbech.
Unlike their predecessors at Colchester in the 1830s, Bury's businessmen were committed to the idea that railways would benefit them,
and supported proposals for a new north-south route through Bury
which it was hoped would give better communication with London.
'When the railway to Thetford and Sudbury opened', declared one of
the traders, 'much commerce would be brought to Bury, and Bury
would yet one day be a far more important town than it had been for
the last 300 years'. This railway was built, but hopes were not fulfilled
by it. By the 1860s, the main lines of railway were already establishing

a pattern of trade, which extra branch and cross-country routes were unlikely to alter.

The market towns which gained most from the railway had good main-line services, as Colchester, Peterborough and Carlisle demonstrate. That did not deter the people of other towns from pinning their faith on small branch lines as likely to revive lost trade and bring new industry, and right until the First World War rural branches were being projected. Southwold, in Suffolk, had been left out when the main line to Lowestoft was built, and after a few false starts a branch was opened in 1879. The entry on Southwold in *Kelly's Directory* shortly afterwards was of the opinion that the new railway would be a boon to the town, 'especially if the fishing trade which has been diverted to Lowestoft and Yarmouth since the opening of the Great Eastern Railway is again revived'. But it was too late, and the fishing trade did not revive. Express trains took the fish from Lowestoft and Yarmouth, whereas all the Southwold Railway could offer was a slow jaunt to meet the main line at Halesworth.

Despite being on a branch line, Abingdon's population increased by about 50 per cent during the nineteenth century. It did, however, start out with over 4,000 people at the beginning of the century, and was one of the three largest towns of Berkshire. Even so, its growth was far less than either Oxford or Reading with main railway lines passing through. The small towns on branch lines, like Southwold, nearly all remained small. Yet at Southwold, too, population rose quite sharply in the 1880s and 1890s after the railway was opened. The town's few industries gained a little, and the railway brought the beginnings of tourism, so that the investment in the line was probably worthwhile. Towns with no railway at all were usually worse off. Odiham, though the railway passed only two or three miles away, lost trade to Basingstoke where the station was within the town. Brough had only its horse fair as a vestige of its former status. Burford was left high and dry in the Cotswolds, its population of 1,725 in 1801 falling to 1,323 by 1901. But isolation was seen as a positive advantage by some. Burford by 1914 had become 'a place which attracts people who choose, and are able, to live where railways and all that they bring are absent'.

=5=
Social Developments

POPULATION

The writer of the entry on Odiham, Hampshire for the *Universal British Directory* of 1796, made the observation that 'in the year 1786 the number of inhabitants was one thousand four hundred and thirty; but population daily increases'. Events did not live up to his expectations, for at the census of 1801 the population of Odiham had reached no more than 1,485, and even at its peak at the 1871 census the number of inhabitants of the town was just 2,833.

The population history of market towns was not always straightforward as the differing influences of transport, industry and the fortunes of agriculture produced diverging experiences, even between neighbouring towns. Basingstoke was slightly less than twice the size of Odiham in the eighteenth century, but by 1914 while Odiham's population was hovering around 2,700, Basingstoke's was up to 11,259 and rising. As these two towns demonstrate, it was during the nineteenth century that the differences became greatest. The great amongst provincial towns tended to become greater; some of the middling towns of 1801 were growing steadily by 1901; but large numbers of humbler places stagnated.

Everywhere, population was growing rapidly during the late eighteenth century and up to about the 1840s. Agriculture was increasing its production through investments in enclosure, the cultivation of waste lands and the growing of new fodder crops (principally clover and turnips), which supported greater numbers of cattle and sheep of better breed. This in turn brought more business and prosperity to the country town, its markets, craftsmen and professional services. There are some examples of rapid growth in the first three decades of the nineteenth century: Horncastle by 98 per cent, Hitchin 65 per cent, Stroud 59 per cent. All of these places were growing at a greater rate than England and Wales as a whole, for which the average was 51 per cent. Small towns, although there were a few exceptions, tended to have slighter increases in population of around 25-30 per cent, and some, like Woodstock and Burford, hardly added any to their numbers. The large market towns, like Colchester with over 11,000 inhabitants in 1801, did not necessarily grow rapidly. Colchester increased its population by only a quarter between 1801 and 1821, then a faster increase in the 1820s took the average for three decades to 40 per cent. The experience of Newark was closely similar.

For great numbers of market towns, population growth stopped at some point between 1831 and 1861. Thereafter, population was either more or less constant or declined. This feature is represented by, for example, Witney and Faringdon, which stopped growing in 1841, and Horncastle, where the peak came in 1851 (*see* Fig 1). It was the small and middling towns that were most affected by this trend. They were the ones with the weaker markets and smaller range of services, and consequently suffered as more rapid transport concentrated these activities. They also had few industries; of these three towns, Faringdon had none, Horncastle had tanning and shoemaking and Witney its blankets, but at neither were these strong enough to sustain a greater population. Thus it was that these towns, small and predominantly agricultural, were caught up in the general movement of population away from the countryside. The attractions of higher incomes in industry were proving too great and people were leaving village and country town alike for the big cities. The loss of population was a real blow: the towns began to lose shops and craftsmen; carriers began to take people to the markets of other towns; status began to be lost. The examples shown in the graph were by no means the worst affected. Dozens of towns never had a population exceeding 2,000. Northleach, in Gloucestershire, was one: the population reached a peak of 1,404 in 1861, and had fallen to 968 by 1901, just 154 greater than the figure in the first census a hundred years before.

The towns which continued to expand until 1914 were those at which the markets, shops and rural services became concentrated. They were usually the ones with stronger industries, but even so, few country towns grew at a rate equal to the national average. Even a great provincial centre like Norwich was adding to its numbers only about half as quickly as the country as a whole during the three

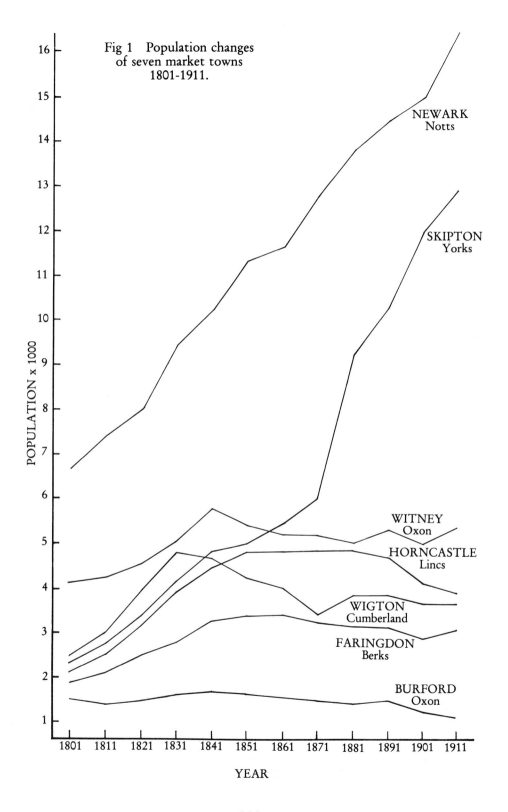

Fig 1   Population changes
of seven market towns
1801-1911.

POPULATION x 1000

16
15
14
13
12
11
10
9
8
7
6
5
4
3
2
1

NEWARK
Notts

SKIPTON
Yorks

WITNEY
Oxon

HORNCASTLE
Lincs

WIGTON
Cumberland

FARINGDON
Berks

BURFORD
Oxon

1801 1811 1821 1831 1841 1851 1861 1871 1881 1891 1901 1911

YEAR

decades before the First World War. The market towns that matched the national rate of growth were those to which a considerable amount of new industry had been attracted during the later nineteenth century. Colchester, with its large-scale clothing trade and engineering works, was one of these. The population here grew by 53 per cent between 1881 and 1911 compared with the average for England and Wales of 38 per cent. Peterborough's growth was similar, sustained by the railways, engineering and brickyards. One of the most remarkable rates of growth was recorded by Leicester. In 1801 it was a small county capital with slightly less than 17,000 inhabitants. By 1911 there were more than 227,000 people living in the town. It was the shoemaking business that was mainly responsible, especially after the introduction of mechanisation in the 1860s. In that one decade, Leicester's population grew by almost 40 per cent, causing the Registrar-General in the report on the 1871 census to remark that 'houses are being rapidly built, and no sooner finished than they are occupied'.

The continued dependence on agriculture is reflected in a slowing of the rate of increase, even a temporary fall in the population figures of a number of towns, during the depression in farming of the last quarter of the nineteenth century. Banbury shared in farming's problems as orders at Samuelson's ironworks dropped. There were labourers out of work in the town, dependent on charitable relief, and a sufficient number left for the town to show a slight fall in population between 1871 and 1881. Cirencester and Newbury were among the other towns experiencing a similar fall in population. Newark fared little better; with its dominant malting industry facing falling demand in the 1880s and 1890s, its population rose by only 6.9 per cent between 1881 and 1901. It was only with the arrival of new engineering businesses late in the 1890s that growth began again.

TOWN PLANNING

The numbers of people living in market towns may not have been growing all that quickly, but they took up more space. Towns everywhere expanded as greater provision was made for housing, for commercial and industrial uses, and for social and recreational needs. Town centres were rebuilt almost completely between 1750 and

1914. Not all towns were equally affected, however. Those stagnant or in decay were altered little and slowly. But all places where commercial, industrial or social life were reasonably active experienced considerable rebuilding in the late eighteenth century, and even more in the nineteenth as the Victorian enthusiasm for civic refurbishment took hold in even the smaller country towns.

Some of the changes made have already been mentioned. Corn exchanges and market halls were built in or near the market-place, sometimes more than once. Ipswich corn exchange built in the 1850s was felt to be inadequate after about thirty years and a replacement was constructed in 1880-2. Hotels were built or rebuilt to accommodate coaching traffic between 1780 and 1830. More were altered, extended or newly built after that, this time to meet business brought in by train. Some of the larger towns had hotels built by the railway companies themselves, for example the Great Northern Hotel at Lincoln, built in 1848.

The most important amongst the other public and commercial buildings put up in the town centre was usually the town hall. Most towns had a hall, often inherited from medieval times, providing covered accommodation for part of the market and a meeting room. Although a few of the new town halls, such as Wokingham, built in 1860, maintained the tradition of providing shelter for market traders, the market was usually accommodated in other ways. Instead the town hall became more of a civic and public building, incorporating a council chamber, a hall for concerts and dances, offices for the town clerk or other chief officers and perhaps court-rooms.

Besides those functions, the town hall was designed to be 'a great ornament to the town', as the one at Sudbury was described. For though the market towns might not be able to emulate Manchester or Leeds in the size of their town halls, a few gained buildings of distinction. Preston, rapidly joining the ranks of industrial towns, employed Sir Gilbert Scott to design its town hall in 1867. Reading's town hall of 1875 was built to the design of Alfred Waterhouse, better known for his work in Manchester. E.W. Godwin produced other notable buildings for the towns of Northampton and Congleton in the 1860s.

The rebuilding of town halls took place at intervals throughout the whole period from 1750 to 1914. Richmond, Yorkshire, was among the towns to build a new hall in the mid-eighteenth century. At

The old town hall at Great Bedwyn, Wiltshire. It was
demolished in the 1870s and not replaced, its markets
unable to compete with nearby Marlborough and Hungerford.

The town hall at Farnham in the 1880s. Built in 1865, it provided
accommodation also for the corn market and assembly rooms.

Hungerford the old Jacobean Court House was replaced by a new town hall in 1786 as the main public assembly room and chamber for manorial courts. This was little bigger than the seventeenth-century building, and in 1870 a larger town hall and corn exchange took its place. Marlborough followed a similar pattern. A town hall was built in 1792-3, but by the closing decades of the following century it had become inadequate, and a replacement was constructed in 1901-2. Most of the new buildings, however, came in the mid-nineteenth century. One of the early decisions of the new Local Board at Farnham was to remove the pleasant, but dilapidated, old market hall and replace it with a town hall which was opened in 1866. Louth, in Lincolnshire, had rebuilt its town hall 'in the Italian style' in 1854. That same year Banbury's new town hall was finished. The old market hall here did not disappear immediately, but was reconstructed as a warehouse by the canal.

There were other new buildings for public authorities, such as the police station. Kesteven magistrates built accommodation for the police at Sleaford in 1845 on the site of some old farm buildings. Gainsborough had a police station in 1843. These two were amongst the earliest. Police forces in the country towns were small and inadequately provided for until well into the nineteenth century. Louth and Wokingham were not unusual in incorporating the police station and cells in the new town halls; separate buildings had to wait for some years.

Private societies and companies provided a number of buildings for public use. There were assembly rooms and reading-rooms, mechanics' institutes and subscription libraries, all of which found sites in the town centre. There were also new commercial buildings, particularly banks, built in the solid styles favoured in the late Victorian and Edwardian years – classical Portland stone or Italianate red brick with stone quoins and mullions. The shops of the large drapers and department stores built from the 1860s onwards added to the imposing, formal styles of the town centre. They also changed the skyline, for the greater number of these buildings were of three storeys or more. The church towers, the ruins of abbeys and castles and one or two public buildings which had formerly stood out, now found themselves competing with the gothic spires of the new town hall, turrets and statues on the corn exchange, and the sheer mass of some of the new shops and public buildings.

Three generations of a market town's police force.

The Assembly Rooms in Boston Market-place, built in 1822.

In these ways, the central streets of country towns were given over more exclusively to public and commercial uses. Tradesmen who had lived over their shops moved out as the larger stores – the furnishers, drapers and department stores – and the branches of multiple retailers moved in, all using the upper floors of the shops for storage. Central houses were converted into offices for solicitors and surgeries for doctors. Towns began to spread outwards.

At first, this was a slow progress. In 1800 most towns were little changed in built-up area since medieval times, and often, like Wareham or Dorchester, were still confined within ancient Saxon or Roman defences. Even towns with reasonable status and population, such as Reading, were little more than a mile across in any direction. Towns where the population had stopped growing by the 1850s or 1860s might stay small in layout until 1914; Chichester spread little beyond its ancient city walls, and Wallingford did not add much to its Saxon site. Stamford was a town that expanded little as a result of restrictions on development imposed by the main landowner, the Marquess of Exeter, as a means of retaining political control.

Towns that were growing began to take up more room during the nineteenth century as new industrial sites were built up and more spacious housing was added to the outskirts of town. Richmond in Yorkshire, recorded a 60 per cent increase in the number of houses

Late nineteenth-century commercial buildings in Sleaford.

between 1801 and 1851, while the population rose only by 43.5 per cent. At Newark over the whole century from 1801 to 1901 the increase in the number of houses exceeded the population's growth, and new residential areas were developed on the edge of the town, especially towards the east. Dorchester began to spread out into the neighbouring parish of Fordington when the open fields there were

The town centre of Ulverston in the early nineteenth century.

enclosed in the 1870s.

The new housing developments took a variety of forms. There were comfortable town houses and villas for the tradesmen and professional classes, and terraces of small brick cottages for the labourers. Increasingly, these types of dwelling were separated, for whereas in 1750 there were streets close to the centre of town where the shopkeeper and the wool merchant might live just a few doors away from a corn porter or a labourer at the soap-boiling works, by 1850 new houses for artisan and employer were built in separate streets, even on opposite sides of the town.

The extension of the town often came in waves corresponding with the changing fortunes of trades and industries. The rising populations of Georgian and Regency times and the air of confidence felt in the markets and trade of so many towns found physical expression in the substantial town houses built at the time. The growth of the textile industry was the stimulus for extensive new building at Wigton in the late eighteenth century. Better known is Chichester, a town which has retained much of the landscape created in this period. Not all the building was new however, behind many an imposing

127

An early nineteenth-century prospect of Newbury. This gives
some indication of the limited extent of the country town before
the railway age.

classical portico and brick facade was a timber-framed house of
seventeenth-century origin. Even though trade might be expanding,
it did not always make the citizens wealthy enough to attain more
than a thin outward show of the modern styles of architecture.

Another phase of the towns' expansion was the second half of the
nineteenth century. New estates and suburbs were laid out, often
stimulated by the presence of the railway. The station itself might be
well outside the town centre, sometimes as far as a mile, and the gap
between railway and town was amongst the first to be filled with new
building. At Hitchin this development was mostly of housing;
Newark went the opposite way as the malt-houses, breweries and
iron foundries advanced along Northgate towards the Great Northern Railway station. At Grantham industry, in particular the
engineering works of R. Hornsby & Sons, moved into the district of
Spittlegate close by the railway. So, too, did the employees, to be near
their work. Spittlegate became an area mainly of new terraced
housing for the industrial workers. By 1911, forty per cent of
Grantham's population lived in this district, compared with eleven
per cent in 1831, when the total was nearly two-thirds smaller.

In 1841-2 the new church of St John the Evangelist was built in

The Parade, Trowbridge. An exceptionally fine row of
eighteenth-century town houses built for the woollen clothiers.

Spittlegate, financed by a subscription fund to which nearly all the
local nobility and gentry contributed handsomely. It was typical of
the towns that were expanding into new suburbs. The Church of
England sooner or later got a building from which to serve the
estates. There was another to the north of Grantham, at Manthorpe,
built in 1847. Banbury gained the churches of St Paul in Neithrop and
Christ Church to the south of the town, both built in the 1850s.
Reading had several new churches as the large parishes that originally
surrounded the town were divided into smaller areas to correspond
with new housing developments.

To these developments were added the Catholic and Nonconformist denominations, whose activities were, if anything, more
vigorous than those of the established church. Their churches and
chapels were built and rebuilt at intervals throughout the period. The
Free Methodists at Grantham took over the former theatre building
before moving to the Congregationalists' old chapel in 1869. The
Congregationalists built themselves a new church, opening in 1870,
while the Roman Catholics, the Baptists and various types of Methodist all constructed churches around the town centre, mainly from

The new Congregational Church built at Boston in 1850.

The interdenominational Mill Street Mission in Dorchester's expanding suburb of Fordington. The photograph dates from 1910.

the 1830s onwards. The smaller towns were hardly less affected by these developments. At Faringdon there was a Baptist chapel, a Congregational church built in 1840, a Primitive Methodist of 1851 and a Wesleyan of 1837.

While most of these developments were covering the ground with bricks and mortar, there were some attempts to create open spaces within the towns. At Dorchester, the remains of the Roman walls around two sides of the town were thrown down in the late eighteenth century to create tree-lined walks for the fashionable to take their promenades. A few other parks, privately owned and almost exclusively for the wealthy, were laid out in the early nineteenth century. Boston had its Vauxhall Gardens, emulating its more famous namesake in London, opened in 1813. The two acres of grounds were laid out in walks, to which a maze modelled on the one at Hampton Court and a marine grotto were added in 1825. Northampton had the Melbourne Gardens, dating from the 1830s. By the middle of the century however, the leisured classes were losing interest in the pleasure gardens. Boston's gardens closed in 1857, and those in a number of other towns followed about the same time. Melbourne Gardens (renamed Franklin Gardens in 1887) kept going, still privately run but increasingly catering for the entertainment of the masses.

New public parks were laid out towards the end of the nineteenth century in the larger towns, arising mainly from a concern to allow open space for the working classes. Boston Corporation opened its People's Park in 1871 at the southern edge of the town. The Albert Park at Abingdon was presented to the town in 1864. There was an Arboretum at Ipswich, and Bedford's park was laid out in the 1880s. Bedford was among the towns to create some space in the central area; St Paul's Square was cleared early in the nineteenth century.

Late in the Victorian years and into the Edwardian, a fashion arose for embellishing towns with drinking fountains and statues. Public subscription funds or the generosity of one or two individuals generally paid for them. The Duke of Bedford presented a statue of John Bunyan to Bedford in 1874. Two years later, a statue of Alfred the Great was erected in the market-place of Wantage through the generosity of Colonel Loyd-Lindsay MP, later Lord Wantage. The likenesses of local notables soon stood in prominent places up and down the land, ranging from the famous Sir Isaac Newton at Grantham and Clive of India at Shrewsbury (he was the town's Member of Parliament 1761-74) to the less well known such as Reverend William Barnes, a Dorsetshire poet, whose statue was erected in Dorchester in 1889.

PUBLIC HEALTH

Not all of the new building took the town out into the fields around it; nor did it necessarily add to the quality of housing. Country towns had numbers of poorly built, run-down cottages. 'The road from the railway station leads through the worst part of the city, presenting long streets and rows of mean houses that impress the mind with the idea of squalid poverty, contrasting strangely with the grandeur of the Cathedral and the Palace' was a comment on Ely in the 1860s. The worst houses were to be found in the courtyards, created by infilling in the town centre, a common practice in the late eighteenth and early nineteenth centuries. At Richmond, seven yards were created behind

Westerham, a small market town in Kent, in 1911. The statue is of
General James Wolfe, the conqueror of Quebec, who was born
here in 1726.

the main streets between the 1770s and 1850 by packing cottages into
the large open plots inherited from the medieval layout of the town.
Kendal was another place where the yards crowded into all available
spaces were a well-known feature, and Alnwick developed in a similar
fashion.

The yards were the poor quarters of the market town, filled with
labouring families. There was a street in Hitchin 'like a slice from the
back slums of Whitechapel, or Kent Street in the Borough. As in the
delectable localities named, at least one house in a half-dozen throughout its length is a lodging home for travellers ...' Besides offering
cheap lodgings, the people of this district found a living by various
forms of labouring, often casual employment, for instance for the
local firm of manufacturing chemists, picking and sorting lavender
and dandelions. The women worked as straw plaiters. Those were
some of the legal occupations. There were others outside the law:
vagrants, pickpockets, prostitutes and thieves all tended to congregate in these run-down corners of town.

Life in the yards was hard, often squalid. Cottages were cramped
and mixed in with town centre businesses such as butchers, grocers
and leather cutters, all of whom tended to make their contributions
to the untidy mess of the open yards. Houses in the yards, whether
new or old, were generally of poor quality. Richmond's medical

officer of health made a number of reports on the town's yards pointing out the number of houses with inadequate light or ventilation, and built below ground level causing them to be uncontrollably damp. The poor quarter of Hitchin had local notoriety; children from the other parts of town were ordered to keep out by their parents for fear of catching some dreadful disease. The main street of the district was indeed called Dead Street until it was decided to give it a more salubrious name in honour of the nation's new monarch; it became Queen Street.

Outsiders were right to be cautious about districts like Hitchin's Queen Street. They were places where disease seemed to strike harder than most other parts of the town. At no time was this more true than during the epidemics of cholera, between the 1830s and 1860s, which struck market towns just as virulently as the industrial centres. Hitchin was affected, as were neighbouring towns in Bedfordshire – Luton, Biggleswade and Bedford – in 1849, the year of the most severe attack of this disease, which affected almost the whole nation. Medical officers, both local and national, pointed to the need to clean up the overcrowded yards. In the aftermath of the 1849 cholera attack, strong reports were made about the conditions in central districts of old towns. Chapman's Yard in Hitchin, with seventeen houses occupied by ninety people had only two privies. Reports on towns in the Lake District did not mince their words. Ulverston was lacking in proper sewers and drains, a mild comment beside the statement that Kendal's overcrowded yards suffered from 'deficiency of all proper drainage ... filth, drunkenness, pauperism, sickness, and an excessive rate of mortality'.

The poor districts with their cramped, ill-ventilated cottages suffered particularly from the lack of public services for water supply and drainage. But in the early nineteenth century, the whole town was little better off. Water for everybody came either from wells or the river. Streams, brooks and ditches which are nowadays culverted, flowed with apparent haphazardness through the back streets carrying sewage and every other kind of waste. George Herbert, a shoemaker from Banbury, in his reminiscences of childhood around 1820, mentions several of these streams. One flowed down Scalding Lane, full of boiling water tipped into it from the soap-boiler's works. Another ran past a dye works, collecting the coloured waste water, to join a couple of other brooks by Water Lane and so to flow into a

Chapman's Yard, off Queen Street, Hitchin. The houses are
badly in need of repair; the yard is muddy; the people are
plainly poor.

ditch too small to manage the supply at peak times. The resultant
floods were the young boys' delight, for they made it impossible to
reach school. The fun of these experiences, though, was far out-
weighed by the general unwholesomeness of the streams, as was
discovered at Boston as late as 1878 when a schoolboy died from
diphtheria which could be blamed with reasonable certainty on the
foul Barditch flowing near the school.

To some extent improvements were under way even before the
medical officers were writing their reports on the 1849 outbreak of
cholera. A start had been made in a few towns towards raising the
standards of the water supply. Boston's water company was formed
in 1845, followed in the next few years by those at Lincoln and
Grantham. By 1850 all three had built their reservoirs and waterworks, and were bringing their pipes into the towns. An energetic
new Board of Health in Banbury encouraged the formation of the
town's water company in 1855; by 1858 it was making its first piped
supplies. Progress elsewhere was often less rapid. By the time the
water started flowing through the pipes at Wigton in January 1869,

fourteen years had passed since the scheme had been proposed. Hungerford's water company was not established until 1903, with a mains service available a year later. At Oakham, in Rutland, in the 1890s water was supplied from 252 wells, a system that was by then hopelessly inadequate and subject to pollution from nearby sewers. But only in 1900 was work on a new piped supply begun.

The provision of better sewerage and drains took longer than bringing piped water to the towns. Banbury was among the more fortunate. Within twenty years of its formation in 1852, the local Board of Health had installed a new system of drainage throughout the town. Elsewhere, the larger towns at least made a start on improving sewage disposal and drainage during the 1860s, but there were those that deferred all attention to this service. Lincoln only started work on a sewerage scheme in 1878 after being forced into it by central government. Even the provision of water pipes and drains did not solve all the problems of the crowded courtyards off Hitchin's Queen Street. The town undertook these improvements in the 1850s, and the death rate and disease did decline. But the houses were still cramped, damp, ill-ventilated and generally in poor condition until they were condemned in the 1920s.

At first sight, it may seem surprising that improvements such as these should have taken so long to carry out, when medical officers reporting on behalf of central government were pointing so forcibly to the need for better conditions. There were those who disputed such conclusions. There was no need for piped water, they would argue, the wells and the old public pump in the market square were good enough – the water coming from them had not killed any of the objectors. Objections along these lines were certainly not without power. They contributed to the delays at Wigton. A resolution that a water company was not necessary at Luton was carried at a public meeting in 1861. There were similar difficulties at Bedford in 1859, and it took another outbreak of typhoid and another investigation by the Privy Council before the town council took the matter in hand. Objections were not silenced even after a water company had been formed. George Herbert at Banbury was incensed when ordered to stop up the wells serving some cottages he owned. He believed the water company was trying to force people to use its services merely to increase its own profits. He sent samples of his well water to King's College, London for analysis and wrote to the *Banbury Guardian* to

publicise the fact that the result was favourable to him. But it was all
to no avail; the company had its way.

More important than objections on the grounds of sheer necessity,
was the problem of whether local authorities should be responsible
for improvements to the fabric, layout and services of the town. Even
more important was the question of how improvements were to be
financed. The fiercest battles raged over how much it would cost to
install mains sewers, piped water, street lighting and the rest. The
strongest objections to the proposals for water companies at Wigton,
Bedford and Luton had all been on the grounds of cost, and the likely
addition to the ratepayers' burden of undertaking such work. It was a
pattern repeated throughout the country, and not on the question of
water supply alone. The ratepayers at Colchester early in the century
had voted down the Channel and Paving Commissioners' plans to
rebuild North Bridge, and restrictions on the Commission's ability
to raise money had likewise prevented its supplying gas to the town in
1817.

Local authorities were often unable or unwilling to become involved in improving their towns for reasons other than those of cost.
By the late eighteenth century, the activities of local government
were minimal to the point of neglect. In the *Universal British
Directory* for 1796, the writer of the entry on Hungerford was of the
opinion: 'The police of Hungerford wants great amendment, the
town is most terribly paved; but this great inconvenience might be
remedied at a trifling expense to the inhabitants, as they have gravel
in such plenty'. Like most market towns, Hungerford was not a
borough, its government was therefore the same as that of any village.
Local decisions were taken by the parish vestry, which had responsibility for the upkeep of public amenities in the town. Members of the
vestries were all part-time, unpaid amateurs, whose duties were a
combination of those of a present-day councillor and his council
official. By the mid-eighteenth century, the limited energies of part
timers for managing the affairs of a town were beginning to make
local government impossible. It was because parish vestries, in both
village and town, were unable to organise the upkeep of the king's
highways as they should have done, that the turnpike trusts had been
formed. Similar things were happening with the management of
other amenities of the town, such as Hungerford's pavements.

Colchester was one of the minority of market towns incorporated by royal charter as a borough, and therefore had its own separate government under a mayor and corporation. Its fellow boroughs like Reading, Grantham or Newark, were generally among the larger places, but there were several which had been granted borough status in the distant past and had not lived up to expectations. Weobly, in Herefordshire, was one, 'a very poor market town, though a Parliament borough', according to Dr Richard Pococke, a bishop in the Church of Ireland who made some lengthy tours of England in the 1750s. The town had two main streets, about 600 inhabitants and little else. There were smaller places, such as Melcombe Regis, one of the notorious rotten boroughs having representation in Parliament but only a handful of electors.

Borough status might have meant that a town was in a better position to improve its amenities, but, in fact, the corporations settled into an inert cosiness, with few duties laid down by the original charter and an unwillingness to take on greater responsibilities. Corrupt, was how the reformers of the early nineteenth century described them, and with reason. Members were not usually elected with the result that these had become self-perpetuating and exclusive bodies. The majority of Marlborough Corporation was made up of representatives from the same half a dozen families for generations. At Colchester the town council, appropriately called the Select Body, was said to spend much of its official income on grand dinners; and the Whig reformers of the 1830s held up Boston as a prime example of a town where the corporation had been used to further the political and social life of its members.

The official duties of the borough corporations were few. They supervised the policing of the town, inspected the prison, managed the markets and administered the properties of the borough and of local charities for which they might act as trustees. Other tasks were neglected or left for others to undertake. The corporations were reformed in 1835 to become properly elected bodies. They began to take a greater interest in the improvement of the towns, and were responsible for several of the changes in market accommodation noticed in earlier chapters. Even so, most activities continued to be the responsibility of private enterprise or other local authorities. Improvement commissioners undertook the maintenance, cleaning and lighting of streets and footpaths, and also had some powers to control new buildings encroaching on to pavements. These powers,

NEW BRIDGE, BOSTON

One of the acts of the unreformed corporation at Boston in 1807
was to build the new cast iron bridge over the River Witham.
Beyond the bridge can be seen the warehouses lining the river
bank almost to the market-place.

with the addition of responsibilities for water supply and sanitation,
were transferred to Local Boards of Health established under the
Public Health Act of 1848. The local boards disappeared in the 1870s
and 1880s when borough councils and, in unincorporated towns, the
urban district councils assumed all these responsibilities.

POWER

Joint stock companies, private subscriptions and sometimes individual beneficence provided corn exchanges, libraries, museums and
assembly halls. Gas was almost always supplied by private enterprise.
The opportunity to build a public gasworks was offered to the
Channel and Paving Commissioners at Colchester in 1817, but when
they were unable to raise the capital required, an independent
company was quickly established. Colchester, in fact, was one of the
first towns in the country to have a gas supply. Chelmsford's came
shortly afterwards, Reading's in 1818 and Chesterfield's in 1825. It
was usually the 1830s and 1840s before gas companies were set up in

market towns. Banbury's was promoted in 1833; Dereham and Sudbury both established companies in 1836, Tewkesbury in 1842 and Hungerford in 1845. By 1850, the larger towns were nearly all supplied, as were several of the smaller ones, including Faringdon, and others were rapidly catching up.

Unlike the supply of water and disposal of sewage, the idea of having gas lighting was generally popular. At Banbury, when the gas company had laid the main pipes throughout the town, there was, recalled George Herbert, 'rejoicing, and a grand illumination with stars of gas, transparencies, and other devices of the usual kind'. Reading had two gas companies for a few years, after complaints from the public about the quality of service from the original Reading Gas Company prompted the formation of the rival Reading Union Gas Company in 1835. The competition apparently had the desired effect of reducing the price and raising the standards of service.

The main use for the gas at first was to light the streets and main public buildings. It took a little while for the number of private customers to build up. As soon as the gas company commenced its business in Colchester, the Channel and Paving Commission started erecting 'handsome cast iron fluted pillars' along the High Street to take the new form of illumination. It was the same everywhere. At Reading, a year after the gas company was formed, the chief streets of the town had their gas lamps turned on for the first time.

Streets had been lit before the gasworks were built. Lighting was one of the principal duties undertaken by improvement commissioners when they were formed towards the end of the eighteenth century. Oil lamps were used. They were installed at Sudbury in 1825, a mark, it was thought, that the town was recovering from the depression following the loss of its woollen industry. Reading's central streets had oil lamps by 1811. They were lit every night between 13 September and 14 April, except for the four nights before and one night after a full moon. No mention was made in the regulations as to what should happen if it was cloudy or even foggy on those nights.

Gas improved the quality of street lighting, but did not necessarily extend its duration. The need for economy meant that it was usual in all towns for lights to be off for the summer. At Reading in 1821, there was even a public subscription which raised nearly £60 to enable the lamps to be lit during those months. In 1837 the Paving Commissioners were pleased to announce that a reduction in the price of gas meant that one-third of the street lamps could be kept alight all year. Even then, the lamps would not be allowed to burn all night, but were put out at midnight, which, as George Sturt recalled of his early years in the wheelwright's shop at Farnham, made getting to work at six o'clock on a winter's morning an interesting, sometimes eerie experience.

By 1914 electric lighting was available. General commercial generation of electricity started in the 1880s. Colchester was quick to take it up. The council granted a concession to a company in 1882 which set up its power station in a former distillery to supply electricity for street lighting and businesses. Use of the new power spread quickly. During the 1890s, local generating companies were established at several of the larger country towns, such as Chelmsford (1890), Oswestry and Shrewsbury (1895), and Lincoln (1898). By the First World War, electricity was available, at least to a limited extent, at a number of small towns. Faringdon was among them, as was Southwold, where electric lighting was one of the luxurious amenities advertised by the Grand Hotel.

CHARITABLE FOUNDATIONS

Care for the sick, the poor and the elderly was the work of private charity throughout this period. All towns had a selection of charitable foundations, some dating from the sixteenth century which provided support in money or in kind to the poor. The more substantial grant in kind was accommodation in cottages and almshouses, but there were smaller endowments providing gifts of coal or clothing. Besides these endowed funds, there were more general charitable activities. Leading landowners and businessmen made individual grants of coal, food or clothing, while the less wealthy of the gentry and middle classes supported the growing number of subscriptions and societies.

Hospitals were charitable foundations until the early twentieth century. At first, there were only one or two hospitals in each county, at principal places, though not always the county town; the Essex Hospital was at Colchester, not Chelmsford. The Shropshire Infirmary at Shrewsbury was one of the first county hospitals, opened in 1745. The Lincoln County Hospital opened in 1769, those at Northampton and Bedford in 1793 and 1803, and the Essex and Colchester Hospital in 1818. Elsewhere, dispensaries were opened from the late eighteenth century, at Horncastle in 1789 and St Albans in 1843, for example. Gradually more places were provided with their own hospitals. A North Hertfordshire & South Bedfordshire Hospital was opened at Hitchin in 1840. The dispensary at St Albans was rebuilt as a hospital in 1870. Luton's hospital was opened in 1882; previous to that there had been a cottage hospital established in two converted houses in 1872. By 1914 there were cottage hospitals at a number of small towns, including Southwold opened in 1897.

The cottage hospital at Faringdon, opened in 1892, was the gift to the town of W. Dundas, Esq., a local landowner. It was the same everywhere. Savernake Hospital at Marlborough, founded in 1866, was on land donated by the Marquess of Ailesbury. Lord Sidmouth gave the site for the Royal Berkshire Hospital at Reading, built between 1837 and 1839. Raising the money for the buildings, and then the rebuildings and extensions, together with the running costs kept the fund raisers occupied throughout the nineteenth century. There were straightforward public subscriptions supported mainly by the gentry and business classes; churches held special collections; the gentry organised balls and bazaars. Later came flag days, and Hospital Saturday became an established feature of urban life.

Principal among charitable foundations of the market town were the schools. A high proportion of towns had endowed grammar schools which had traditionally acted as educational centres for the town and the villages. They were failing in this by the beginning of the nineteenth century and standards were commonly falling. The numbers of pupils were also falling, and some schools closed. Colchester Grammar School was open only in name for some years around 1800. Carre's School at Sleaford remained closed for about twenty years after 1816. In 1834, however, the school was revived. It was rebuilt and a new master's house added. This was a pattern followed by many ancient schools in country towns. Their standards and fortunes revived, especially from the mid-nineteenth century. Some, like Marlborough, became major public schools and an important influence upon the town, but everywhere the school contributed to cultural and sporting life. Besides the endowed schools, there were private academies established mainly to educate the children of

The Savernake Hospital at Marlborough, from a postcard of about 1907.

tradesmen in the town. Nonconformists had a few secondary schools of their own. As standards and interest in education increased during the later nineteenth century, a number of new schools were established. In particular, at the end of the period high schools for girls were founded, for instance at Lincoln in 1892, Colchester in 1909 and Grantham in 1910.

There was little provision for primary education for the children of the poor and lower middle classes in the late eighteenth century. There were various private schools run by clergymen and some 'dame schools', but they were small and few in number. Charity and church schools existed in a few towns, such as the Bluecoat School at Colchester, and from the 1780s Sunday schools were founded by most churches.

During the early nineteenth century, the provision of elementary schools increased rapidly everywhere as both Anglican and Nonconformist churches set up new day-schools. The Anglicans' National Society for Promoting the Education of the Poor was founded in

1811, and by the 1840s was represented in almost all towns. The Nonconformists were less wealthy and could support fewer schools. The Methodists had only three schools in the towns of Lincolnshire in the 1840s, and the Baptists had one at Boston. The state gave financial assistance to the schools run by the churches from the 1830s, and after the Education Act of 1870 itself undertook the provision of schooling, through the establishment of School Boards. It did not make an immediate change to the education of many market towns, however. Most avoided setting up School Boards, preferring the existing mixture of church and private schools. St Albans was unusual amongst the towns of Hertfordshire in having two Board schools by 1886. Berkhamsted and Hemel Hempstead had established School Boards in the 1870s, Watford joined them in 1883, but other towns still had no state school. It was the same in Lincolnshire; Grimsby School Board was formed by 1874, Boston's in 1894, but no other town in the county was keen.

Despite all the problems of establishing efficient authorities and all the arguments over finance, the fabric of the market town was improved immeasurably by 1914. Streets which had commonly been full of pot-holes and unevenly paved in 1800, now had good surfaces, whether of cobbles, asphalt or stone slabs. They were lit, usually by gas, but in the larger towns, Colchester and Lincoln among them, electric lighting had been installed from the late 1890s. The towns now had good water supply and sewerage systems; public cemeteries had been opened; some of the activities that might be hazardous to health, such as the cattle markets and slaughterhouses, were being removed from the town centre. In all, the market towns had been tidied up. In some respects perhaps, they were being made too neat. The people of Farnham were missing their old market hall, which had gone in the early years of the Local Board of Health, and at Pickering there were many who thought the authorities were being too zealous when they cleared the old stocks out of the town centre.

The physical changes were a considerable achievement for small towns, made, as most were, in a period no longer than thirty or forty years. The wrangles over finance, indeed, were often less the result of meanness, as they might appear to be, than the fact that a sum like the £8,000 which the sewers at Beccles were to cost in the 1860s, was no small amount to be found. Add to that similar sums for a waterworks, gasworks and other amenities, and it becomes clear that the joint stock companies were often the best means of raising the money, rather than pressure on the unwilling ratepayers. As local government was placed on a surer footing, the councils began to take over the public services. Richmond Borough Corporation was among the early ones, buying the gasworks there in 1849, but most towns took this step from the 1870s and 1880s.

=6=
Market Town Culture

FAIRS AND FESTIVITIES

It has been mentioned more than once that fairs and markets were more than business meetings. They were almost always social occasions, on however small a scale. There were the casual gatherings of farming people around the market-place and in the inns, and there were the more formal market dinners. For the womenfolk, the retail market was sometimes as much a source of free entertainment from the stallholders with their extravagant patter as it was a serious shopping excursion. The truly recreational occasions, though, came at the major fairs in the market town's calendar.

Farnham had three fairs: one in May, one on Midsummer's Day and a third in November. Of these, the Midsummer Fair was the pleasure fair, although in George Sturt's memories of childhood, 'they all alike seemed to me opportunities for shouting men to drive horses, cattle, and especially sheep'. But there was far more to it. Whereas the spring and autumn fairs may have had a few side-shows and bazaars, it was the Midsummer Fair that had the most. The whole host of delights filled Castle Street: the stalls selling gingerbread; the peepshows; the travelling menageries; the fat, thin, small, bearded and other misshapen ladies; the coconut shies, swing-boats, cakewalks and roundabouts. After the shouting men had finished their morning's business of driving hard bargains over the horses, cattle and sheep, the entertainments took over and continued late into the evening.

It was the same at all market towns. The fun-fair came in all its glory once or twice a year. The statute fairs were commonly occasions for the pleasure fair, since by tradition the hiring day was a holiday for the labourers in yearly service. They had been paid their last year's wage, and the showmen were only too willing to help them spend a

146

A small roundabout at a country fair illustrated in
W.H. Pyne's *The Costume of Great Britain*, published in 1804.

little of it – much to the disgust of local newspaper reporters who
would regularly comment that the labourers had come more for the
amusements than for the serious business of finding employment.
Other occasions for pleasure fairs were often the general produce
fairs like that at Sturbridge. Gradually, the pleasure fair came to take
over these occasions, although the salesmen of toys, novelties and
cheap manufactured goods such as drapery and crockery never
entirely disappeared.

As the pleasure fair grew larger, its entertainments became more
extravagant. Farnham fairs in the 1860s consisted largely of the
various spectacles such as strong ladies, conjurers and wrestling
booths. There were old-fashioned Aunt Sallies and newer coconut
shies. There were several peepshows, which George Sturt remem-
bered as disappointing – with their meagre views of such scenes as the

Relief of Lucknow or Queen Victoria's Coronation. Menageries were always popular in the early nineteenth century, catering as they did for the public's taste for the unusual and fantastic. They used all the showman's razzmatazz to draw in the crowds. 'Wombwell's Menagerie', seen by William Howitt at the Nottingham Goose Fair, had a brass band dressed in beefeaters' costumes to attract attention to the show.

There were swings and roundabouts as well, and it was these that became the dominant feature of the fairground by 1914. The small roundabouts of the early part of the period, turned by hand or horses, were replaced by magnificent affairs with their gaudily carved galloping horses and ostriches, three or four abreast. Steam-engines drove the roundabout; they drove dynamos to produce electricity for the gaily-coloured lights; and they powered the mechanical organs attached to roundabouts and other rides. Steam roundabouts first appeared in 1865 and grew ever more elaborate until by 1911 there were fourteen different types of joy-ride at St Giles's fair in Oxford, ranging from gallopers to 'scenic railways'. By this time, the joy-rides were being challenged for their place as pride of the fair by the new bioscopes, moving picture shows which attracted excited attention with their mammoth organs, parades of dancers and the films of various dramatic events.

These fairs were major events in the market town's calendar, looked forward to for weeks. Fair day itself was often a holiday in the town, and schools were closed, as were many of the businesses. But these were also occasions for the villagers, who came streaming in on foot, by carrier's wagon or by train. Excursion trains to Oxford for St Giles's fair were run from as far away as Birmingham in 1859, and the *Oxford Times* reported that in the evening, the Great Western Railway's station was 'literally besieged' by a crowd of 3,000-4,000 waiting to go home. There was something for everybody at the fairs. Though they were predominantly entertainment for the masses, there could be attractions for more fashionable classes. The afternoon of the Nottingham Goose Fair into the mid-nineteenth century was the 'gig fair' when, wrote William Howitt, 'smart people from all quarters come to see and to be seen'. This fair was one lasting for more than one day, so the done thing amongst these people was to come on the second day.

'Joy . . . to all fair goers' was William Howitt's considered opinion,

Marlborough Mop Fair in the High Street of the town. This is from a postcard of the 1920s, when the large mechanical rides were still little changed from those introduced in the late nineteenth century.

but it was not shared universally amongst the respectable people of town. The boisterousness did not always meet with approval. The free association of young people with members of the opposite sex, led to fairs being criticised for their immorality. The ladies at Lincoln opened the corn exchange as a room of rest and refreshment for young girls at the hiring fairs on a number of occasions in the late nineteenth century. The second ground of complaint about fairs was the number of criminals attracted into the town by the large crowds. It was a problem as old as the fairs themselves. With 10,000 people said to have been at Abingdon's October statutes in 1805, the pickpockets had a field day while the crowd's attention was held by the spectacles of the Grand Turk's Palace and the Little Strong Woman. In 1834 the newspaper returned to the same theme in its report this time on the June fair at Abingdon: 'prostitutes, pickpockets, highwaymen, footpads, and swindlers, made a much larger display than usual'. One might imagine from this that they were an attraction with as much fanfare as the travelling menagerie.

Reports on the problems of criminal activity at fairs around the country appeared regularly in the local press throughout the nineteenth century. Mid-Victorian concern for propriety led to pressure to have fairs stopped altogether. Some of the old pedlary fairs

Jack in the Green, a traditional festival of May Day, taking
place in this illustration of 1843 around the market cross.

succumbed to this pressure; so too, did a number of statute fairs as
their business of hiring servants disappeared. Wellingborough's was
one of these, abandoned in the early 1870s. There were as many
others though, like Barnet fair, which would not be suppressed. St
Giles's fair in Oxford, which grew from being a tiny festival at the end
of the eighteenth century into the greatest fun-fair for the people of
Oxfordshire by 1900, survived an attempt to have it abolished in
1894.

The fair was the highlight of the year for the mass of the population
of the market town and its surrounding villages. There were other
traditional activities continuing well into the nineteenth century,
some to the end of the period. May Day was one of the more prolific
occasions for these festivities. The various forms of traditional
dancers were out, such as the morris men and sword-dancers. Hobby-
horses were part of the tradition in places such as Minehead, and
Helston's famous furry dance took place on about 8 May. Plough
Monday, Lammastide, Easter and Guy Fawkes Day were all occasions when traditional celebrations might take place. Not all were
purely entertainments for the common people. Hungerford had a

celebration at Hock-tide (just after Easter) for the election of the new town constable. The constable was escorted by two 'tutti men', who, once that part of their duties was over, paraded round the town, calling on every house demanding a coin from the men and a kiss from the women, in exchange for which they handed over an orange.

Wakes and revels had their origins as watch-night ceremonies on the holy day of the saint to whom the parish church was dedicated. These were still kept up quite generally at the end of the eighteenth century as two or three days of general jollification. A wide variety of activities was associated with wakes, from simple games and bonfires to donkey racing, wrestling matches or mock elections in caricature of the town's authorities. These were events which often attracted itinerant sellers of novelties, gingerbread, cakes and so on, who set up their stalls for the few days. Jugglers, acrobats and other small-time performers were also likely to appear, and out of this mixture of people and events a bigger fun-fair might emerge. This was the origin of St Giles's fair at Oxford. That transformation was far from universal. Oswestry represents the opposite trend, where by the 1850s the old ways of celebrating wakes, with feasts and games, were simply dying out.

SPORT

Among the activities once common at wake festivals were prize-fights, bull-baiting and cock-fighting. Respectable opinion, led mainly by the evangelical churches, turned against these sports, especially the last two. An Act of 1835 banned bull-baiting and made it illegal to own a cockpit, but failed to stop the sport so that further legislation was necessary in 1849. These blood sports had been important in the recreational life of the country. Bull-baiting was widely popular; Congleton in Cheshire and Wokingham in Berkshire were just two of the towns particularly noted for this activity, which was by no means confined to wake feasts. It was a popular part of the Guy Fawkes Day celebrations at Lincoln and at Axbridge, in Somerset. At Wetherby, there was a bull-baiting on the occasion of the swearing-in of the mayor each year. Stamford had a particularly well-known variation of the sport, a bull running, held every 13 November. A bull was released to run the length of the main street, its progress being interrupted by repeated torments from as many as were prepared to show off their daring. This event gained additional notoriety from its blatant disregard of the law passed in 1835. It was not suppressed until 1839 when twenty men of the Metropolitan Police and a contingent of dragoons were sent to enforce a law which the local authorities were unwilling to uphold. The leading citizens and neighbouring gentry were in favour of the sport, the town clerk declaring that the people ought not to be deprived of an entertainment enjoyed in the town for 600 years.

Cock-fighting also continued clandestinely after it was banned, the more easily because the birds could be smuggled into the yards at the back of an inn, to show off their prowess before a carefully invited audience. While it was legal this sport was big business. Tournaments were arranged between representatives of neighbouring towns and betting on the outcome of the fights was heavy. The local paper at Oxford carried a notice in April 1834 for one such meeting between Wantage on one side, Abingdon and Oxford on the other. Three battles were fought at £10 a battle, Wantage winning by two to one. With stakes so high, this was clearly an activity not confined to the masses. Like bull-baiting, it enjoyed support from the rich and respectable, including a parson at Petworth who 'enjoyed a set-to between the services', as a resident of the town later recalled.

The interest taken by the wealthy in cock-fighting is a small indication of the extent to which the gentry led the cultural and recreational life of the market town in the eighteenth century and the first half of the nineteenth. They, after all, had the money and time to indulge in such activities. So it was, that when respectable opinion began to turn against bull-baiting and cock-fighting it became possible to legislate against them. Lord Egremont, for instance, was set against cock-fighting in 'his' town of Petworth. It is fair to suppose that the labouring classes would have been quite happy to continue cheering on fights and adding their pence to the bets.

The gentry and the employers in the towns fostered the new sports that were later to have mass appeal. This was especially true of cricket which was played in the eighteenth century almost exclusively by the landed classes. Matches celebrated in the annals of the game were arranged between teams representing the gentlemen of England and those of Sussex or Hampshire. Betting was so heavy on some of these matches as to make the sums staked on cock-fighting seem like pocket-money. During the 1790s, a club at Maidenhead played matches against the All-England team and the Marylebone Cricket Club for £100 a match. A 'Grand Cricket Match' in 1829 between the MCC and Bury St Edmunds was for 1,000 guineas.

By the 1820s and 1830s cricket clubs, mainly patronised by the gentry and middle classes, were being formed at market towns all round the country. Chelmsford's club was founded in 1825, Sleaford's in 1834, and those at Banbury and Kendal in 1836. It was the wealthy who provided the cricket grounds as well. The cricket club at Macclesfield, founded in the 1830s, played for many years in the grounds of Ryle's Park, the mansion of the Ryle family, leading silk and cotton spinners in the town.

During the second half of the nineteenth century, cricket began to involve a wider range of people. Bernhard Samuelson at Banbury was one of those who took a lead by providing fields and organisation for teams from amongst the workers at his iron foundries. It was an example followed by other large employers. By the end of the century, there were several agencies through which sport could be organised as can be seen from the names of some of Marlborough's cricket clubs: St Mary's, Congregational Church, Liberal Club and Working Men's Club.

A similar pattern was followed in the organisation of other sports. The traditional form of football, played in the streets between teams of as many who came, had been common in market towns. It continued through the nineteenth century at quite a few places, including Corfe Castle in Dorset, Alnwick in Northumberland, Ashbourne in Derbyshire and Atherstone in Warwickshire. The modern forms, played to the rules of Rugby or the Football Association, emerged in the second half of the nineteenth century. Again the initiative in organising clubs was at first taken by the gentry, employers and schools, before gaining wider support through the churches, working men's clubs and other similar groups. Most other sports were organised: athletics from the mid-nineteenth century, tennis from the 1870s. Golf and cycling both achieved widespread popularity during the last two or three decades of the century.

Swimming was a form of exercise popular from the eighteenth century. Townspeople at places on the coast or by rivers took a dip whenever they could. There were some at least who did not confine swimming to the warm seasons of the year. Alderman Blandy of

153

Reading was drowned in December 1817 when, so the inquest was told, he went for his customary bathe in the river. Reading was among the few towns to build swimming baths early in the nineteenth century. They were opened in 1834, fed with water from the River Thames, and proved so popular that new, larger baths were built in 1843. Boston also had baths opened in 1834, but generally the provision of pools came later, mainly from the 1870s onwards.

Horse-racing was another of the market town's sports that had wide popular appeal, but which relied to a considerable extent on gentry patronage. Some races were almost entirely events of the masses, associated usually with horse fairs and cattle fairs at which the dealers, drovers and gypsies would organise scratch competitions. The Welsh drovers' races at Barnet fair became a noted feature every year until 1871 when the railway line was built across the course. Other race meetings were almost exclusively events for the gentry. Newmarket was principal amongst those which discouraged the general public from attending. Most races, however, were between such extremes. They were popular events, attended by a large proportion of the town's population admitted freely – entrance charges being rare. The crowds were able to cheer on the half-bred horses entered by the farmers and small tradesmen, and the thorough-breds of the landowners, such was the general mixture of events at meetings until the railway age. It was the nobility and gentry, however, who undertook the organisation of the meetings. The list of stewards at Abingdon's races in the late eighteenth century reads like a roll-call of local nobility, with the Lords Abingdon, Harcourt, Craven and their neighbours regularly taking on this office. Financial support came from the landowners and wealthy townsmen who would each subscribe to collections for the prize money. Marl-borough was typical in that on the two days of its races, the first comprised competitions for the noblemen's and gentlemen's plate, the second for the town plate.

The great majority of market town race-meetings of the eighteenth and early nineteenth centuries were purely local affairs. The motley collection of horses and events was a measure of this, for at most places there were simply not enough good horses available. So the farmers' and butchers' nags were only too welcome, and to spin the competitions out to fill the two or three days of the meeting, a system of heats was often organised. Race-meetings could be intermittent in

The races at Reading depicted by the *Illustrated London News* on the occasion of the revival of racing there in 1844.

their occurrence. In Oxfordshire there were races at Burford, Oxford, Bicester, Woodstock and a few smaller places, but in some years of the early nineteenth century only one or two of these took place. Shortage of horses was a major reason. Sometimes rival attractions drew people away, 'excursions to sea ports' being one thing blamed for the poor attendance at Abingdon's races in 1794. Reading's races disappeared for several years when the heath on which they had been run was enclosed in 1814. The conditions under which races were run were sometimes far from ideal by modern standards. In 1828 torrential rain at Abingdon meant that 'the course was in such a state that the horses had to run for some distance up to their knees in water; and the appearance of the jockeys at the end of each race was truly ludicrous; they were completely covered with mud, and not a feature could be recognised'.

These were social occasions rather than serious sporting events. People were there for the fun of the race and for the side-shows. The common people had various revels alongside the races; the gentry had cock-fights. The Gentlemen of Berkshire would take on the Gentlemen of Wiltshire and other counties in cock-fights at Abingdon, the stakes for these being very high. After the races, the leisured classes would retire to one of the inns in town for a lavish meal, inappropriately called an ordinary, followed by dancing late

155

into the night.

The railways had a dramatic effect on racing. For one thing, they brought larger crowds to the meetings. The companies were quick to lay on special trains: almost as soon as the line to Kingston-upon-Thames was opened in 1838, the London and Southampton Railway ran trains to the Derby, for which there was an overwhelming demand. The influx of visitors was not always welcomed. The Jockey Club tried every ruse to maintain the exclusive character of New-market. At Oxford, where the races had always been open, the local police and the university began to complain that excursion trains from the large cities were filling the town with undesirables. The second effect of the railways was that horses could travel more easily, so that the supply of talent at meetings need not be restricted to the immediate locality. The ability to move people and horses to races over greater distances had the effect of concentrating racing at fewer, larger meetings. The old social events began to die away. Racing was becoming a more serious business, a mass spectator sport.

From the 1870s enclosed racecourses, such as Sandown Park and Newbury, were set up, owned by private companies, who charged entrance fees to all visitors. There was no room for the amateur racing between the horses of farmers and landowners here. Not only were the market town events the poor relations, unable to compete with the professional sport, but the gentry and townsmen lost interest in organising events which the excursionists from major cities were likely to overwhelm. Thus, from the 1840s, the once or twice yearly racing festivities at market towns began to disappear. Reading's went in 1875, and those at Oxford and Abingdon were other casualties.

The gentry had sports of their own, which often had bases in the market towns. Until the end of the nineteenth century, Melton Mowbray was probably more important as a centre for fox-hunting than for its pork pies. With four packs meeting here, landed society gave the town a special character during the hunting season, from November till early April. Much of the town's business was directed towards the hunting fraternity, with several hotels offering accom-modation for huntsmen and their families, and stabling for their horses. The same was true of a number of towns in the Midlands. Bicester was described in 1916 as 'a pretty little town which devotes itself mainly to serving the needs of people who farm and hunt', the local pack being one of the best in the county. A few towns were noted as centres for fishing, Ellesmere in Shropshire, for example, with the lakes just outside.

Until the middle of the nineteenth century, the cultural activities of the market town were determined largely by the patronage of the gentry. They had the combination of leisure, education, wealth and interest enough for literary institutions and theatres to be successfully established. The gentry, however, did not bestow their favours equally on all towns. Most were neglected, while a minority became quite genteel. Indeed, a few towns apparently were little else but service centres for the wealthy. The early directories describe Maidenhead as having little commerce, but a good general trade from the large number of rich people living nearby. The mainstay of the life of Dorchester, thought Dr Pococke in the 1750s, was 'the thoroughfare to Exeter, and the nobility and gentry who live near it'.

The gentry had certain business affairs to bring them into country towns. They were connected mainly with legal and administrative matters, the assizes and quarter sessions. There was also business connected with county regiments of militia and yeomanry, which had their bases in the larger market towns; and there were political meetings demanding the attention of the leading landowners. Whatever the need for visiting the town, the nobles and gentry were always apt to mix business with pleasure, so that race-meetings, dances and visits to the theatre were often arranged to coincide with the assizes and other major events. The county towns and one or two of the other more prominent places were the centres for these activities.

Among the highlights of the social calendar for the landed classes was the annual ball. One was held in the Red Lion at Banbury each January for the local nobility. The 'Stuff Ball' at Lincoln became a major county event. It was originally a Lincolnshire protest against the growing strength of the cotton industry, for all ladies attending had to wear a garment of wool (or 'stuff') to show support for the county's sheep farmers. By the 1830s that rule had gone, but the ball remained as a great social occasion. Besides these main annual dances, there were others on a more occasional basis, again likely to be associated with other interests of the landed classes. A Volunteers' Ball took place at Sleaford in 1864, attracting 230 to attend.

LIBRARIES

Among the pursuits of the leisured classes of the eighteenth century was an interest in literature. Gentlemen's clubs, subscription libraries and reading-rooms were founded to further that interest. An early example was the Spalding Gentlemen's Society, dating from 1712. It held weekly meetings to read and discuss the newspapers of the day, the *Tatler* and the *Spectator* especially, a more formal arrangement for the type of literary and political discussion that otherwise took place in coffee-houses. Wisbech had a similar society formed shortly afterwards, and a few other towns of the eastern counties followed later. Subscription libraries were opened first in the main provincial centres, such as Liverpool, Manchester and Sheffield, in the middle of the eighteenth century. Smaller country towns in the north followed soon after: the library at Warrington was established in 1760, at Leicester and Carlisle in 1761, Stockton on Tees and Ulverston both in the 1770s, and Kendal in 1794. By the end of the century subscription libraries were to be found widely across the country. All of these libraries were for the wealthy, who paid an annual subscription of as much as ten shillings. There was some provision for other classes in the later eighteenth century. Kendal was exceptional in having its Economical Library, founded in 1797, which was mainly for the working classes, but usually they had to wait until mechanics' institutes were founded twenty to thirty years later before they had libraries or reading-rooms.

The professional and trading classes sometimes formed their own book clubs. There were some in existence by 1750, usually founded by clergymen. The George Book Club at Huntingdon was one; Boston had another. The numbers grew rapidly in the 1780s and 1790s, partly as a result of the exciting politics of the times, which a wide range of country town people wanted to read about. Besides these clubs, there were private libraries run as a business venture, mostly by printers and stationers.

The provision of libraries for the labourers, artisans, clerks and small tradesmen of the market town remained limited until the beginning of the twentieth century. Private libraries and those of such organisations as mechanics' institutes were usually small. A Libraries and Museums Act was passed in 1845 enabling local autho-

CIRCULATING LIBRARY,

OPPOSITE

THE OLD CROWN INN,

PENRITH;

MATTHEW SOULBY most respectfully informs his Friends and the Public, that he continues to augment his CIRCULATING LIBRARY, by the latest Editions of valuable and entertaining Novels, Romances, Voyages, Travels, &c.

The Readers of his Library may be assured of being liberally supplied with the best Modern Publications, conducive to Information, Amusement, and useful Instruction.

Grateful to a discerning Public for the Patronage he has hitherto experienced, M. SOULBY will persevere in the utmost exertion to merit a continuance of Favors.

§ A General Catalogue of the Circulating Library may be had on application.

J. SOULBY, Printer, Ulverston.

A handbill dated 1807 for Matthew Soulby's private library in Penrith.

rities to set up public libraries, but they were unhurried in taking up such powers. Canterbury did so in 1847, Winchester in 1851 and Ipswich in 1853, but on the whole it was late in the nineteenth century before country towns began to establish public libraries. Chesterfield and St Albans took up their powers under the Act in the 1870s, Reading in the 1880s, Colchester and Worksop in the 1890s. Large numbers of new public libraries were built in the Edwardian years. The initiative, though, came from outside the local authorities. Andrew Carnegie put some of the millions he had made in the American steel business into building libraries in the United Kingdom. By the time of his death in 1919, there were 380 of them at places of all sizes throughout the kingdom. Boston, Gainsborough and Stamford were the old towns in Lincolnshire to receive libraries through this generosity, and the library at Lincoln, opened in 1895, was given a new building in 1913.

ENTERTAINMENT

In February 1753 the *Oxford Journal* announced that Mr Linnet's company of comedians would shortly be arriving at Abingdon, after a stay at Wallingford, and would be performing a number of plays in the town hall. This was nothing extraordinary, similar notices appeared at least once a year, for by the 1750s the visits of strolling players were established features of entertainment in the market towns. The companies stayed for about a week at each town performing their repertoire of currently popular works. The entertainment could at best be described as middle-brow. Shakespeare was a standard part of the repertory, with works such as the *Merry Wives of Windsor*, *Henry IV* and *Hamlet*, though not necessarily the whole of the plays. To these might be added adaptations, such as the *Humours of Sir John Falstaff*, which was among the items Mr Linnet brought to Abingdon. The work of Sheridan, the *Beggar's Opera* and *She Stoops to Conquer*, also featured regularly. To those were added numerous farces and melodramas, mainly of one act, which survive now as little more than their titles. The *Farce of the Mock Election* was amongst the repertoire of a company visiting Abingdon in 1764, and 'the much-admired comedy of *John Bull*' was performed at Dunstable in 1804.

THEATRE-ROYAL, ULVERSTON.

On *FRIDAY* Evening the 26th of *DECEMBER*, 1806,
Their MAJESTIES' Servants
Will perform a favourite *TRAGEDY*, called

JANE SHORE.

This excellent Play is undoubtedly the best production of the pathetic ROWE. It contains, among other Historical Passages, the ambitious Schemes of the Duke of Glo'ster, (afterwards RICHARD the III.) to obtain the THRONE, by the cruel Murder of his young Nephews,— the tragical Death of the gallant HASTINGS.—and the almost unparalleled repentance, sufferings, and dreadful end of the beauteous JANE SHORE, whose unhappy Husband is dragged to an ignominious Death, for being caught in the pious office of administering Pardon to her departing Spirit.

Duke of Glo'ster,	Mr. CLIFTON,		Porter,	Mr. DUNNING,
Lord Hastings,	Mr. BUTLER,		Servant,	Mr. WORRALL,
Belmour,	Mr. GEORGE,		Dumont,	Mr. SMITH.
Ratcliffe,	Mr. DAVIS,			
Catesby,	Mr. BEVERLEY,		Alicia,	Miss CRAVEN,
Bishop of Ely,	Mr. MARTIN,		Jane Shore,	Mrs. BUTLER.
Earl of Derby,	Mr. WATSON,			

A *favourite SONG*, by Mr. DUNNING, called

MADAM FIG'S GALA;
Or, *THE YORKSHIRE CONCERT.*
A *favourite SONG*, by Mr. WATSON, called
"*THE POST CAPTAIN.*"
A favourite SONG, by Mr. DAVIS, called
Captain Wattle and Miss Roe.
To which will be added an entire new PANTOMIME, (last time,) called

MOTHER SHIPTON
Or, HARLEQUIN SALAMANDER.

Herlequin,	Mr. DUNNING,		Witches, Messrs.	DAVIS, WATSON,
Pantaloon,	Mr. SMITH,			MARTIN, &c.
Lover,	Mr. JEFFERSON,		Zany Zealous, (*the clown*)	Mr. MEADOWS.
Frenchman,	Mr. GEORGE.			
Tailor,	Mr. BUTLER,		Mother Shipton,	Mrs. MURRAY,
Barber,	Mr. WORRALL,		Columbine,	Miss JEFFERSON.
Doctor,	Mr. CLIFTON,			

IN THE COURSE OF THE PANTOMIME

MOTHER SHIPTON'S CAVE.

Harlequin Rises out of a Cauldron of Fire,
The Magic Guide Post,
A VIEW OF THE WELL HOUSE,
WHICH CHANGES
TO THE DROPPING WELL,
AT KNARESBOROUGH.
THE MAGIC CHAIR.
The celebrated Dying Scene of Harlequin,
And the Skeleton, from Doctor Faustus.
THE WHOLE CONCLUDES WITH A VIEW OF
Mother Shipton's Garden, &c. &c.

BOXES 3s.—PIT 2s.—GALLERY, 1s.——To begin at *Seven o'Clock.*
. TICKETS Delivered where places for the BOXES are Taken, at Mr. SOULBY's Shop, *King-street.*
TICKETS to be had of Mr. BUTLER, at CAPTAIN NEAL's Cavendish-street, and of Mr. ASHBURNER, Printer,
☞ Servants to be sent to keep Places.
On Saturday Evening, the Comedy of the *Wheel of Fortune*, with *Valentine and Orson.*
J. Soulby, Printer, Ulverston.

A playbill from Ulverston for 1806. *Jane Shore* was included in the repertoire of many touring companies of the time.

The town hall as the venue for Mr Linnet's company at Abingdon was nothing out of the ordinary. Indeed, the town hall was one of the better places the players had to perform in. Makeshift theatres were commonly set up in barns and granaries. At Tewkesbury, companies visiting during the summer were accommodated in one of the town's malt-houses, for which this was the close season of operation. Even more temporary theatres in tents, with stages that were sometimes literally collapsible, might be used. Among the visitors to Abingdon in June 1771 was a group of 'ingenious and extraordinary performers' who set up a booth in Ock Street where they were to perform such feats as 'stiff rope dancing, and several balances on the slack wire, without a counterpoise'.

From the mid-eighteenth century permanent theatres began to be built in country towns, often the result of patronage by leading members of the landowning and business classes. William Ormsby-Gore, Esq. built the theatre at Oswestry early in the nineteenth century. Before that there had been buildings at such places as Stamford, Grantham (1800), Reading (1788), Bungay, Beccles (1784) and Chichester (1791), and at Tewkesbury the players were able to move out of the barns and malt-houses into a proper theatre in 1823.

Soon, however, the tide was to turn against such ventures. Puritanism was beginning to dominate the respectable classes of the town; the theatre and dancing were branded as immoral. Since the richer trade and professional people formed the bulk of those who could afford to attend the plays, their change of attitude brought about a decline in the size of audiences. The *Colchester Gazette* for 1 August 1835, noted with some satisfaction in its column for Chelmsford that, 'few respectable people are ever found within the walls of country theatres', and those who did go, did so surreptitiously to avoid notice by their fellows. The reason was simple according to this reporter: 'Men are not such fools as to expend their time and money in seeing men and women make fools of themselves'.

The resident company of Chesterfield theatre surrendered its tenancy in 1838 because the houses were now so empty that huge arrears of rent had built up. The corporation, which owned the building, spent some years considering what to do with it, but eventually it was allowed to continue as a theatre a while longer. Mr Ormsby-Gore's theatre at Oswestry was little used by the 1850s, and dozens of others had also been closed. Richmond's had been converted into wine cellars and an auction room in 1848. Only two of Lincolnshire's towns, Lincoln and Stamford, still had their theatres in 1850, and Stamford's only lasted until 1871 when it became a billiards hall. The players were left to return to their temporary venues, although not necessarily to the barns and warehouses. By this time, however, there were corn exchanges and public assembly rooms available for use as theatres and concert halls, and it was at these that performances were usually put on until late in the century, when new theatres were built in some of the larger towns. Her Majesty's Theatre was opened at Carlisle in 1874, the Lyceum in Ipswich was built in 1890-1, the Grand at Luton in 1898. Northampton retained its Theatre Royal throughout. In 1884 a New Theatre Royal replaced the old, and the opening week featured a familiar selection of *Twelfth Night*, *She Stoops to Conquer* and *School for Scandal*.

Although an influential part of the town turned against the theatre, it did not entirely disappear. Some companies still visited, and from the middle of the nineteenth century amateur societies began to arise. Banbury had a Shakespearian Amateur Society by the 1850s, supported by the Mechanics' Institute. Until the late part of the century, however, these theatrical efforts were small in comparison with the interest in amateur music-making. This was regarded as an uplifting activity and therefore had the support of those opposed to the theatrical companies.

Interest in music took a great variety of forms. George Herbert, the shoemaker and photographer at Banbury, was an active musician, playing with friends in chamber groups. Banbury had a choral society from 1844 and a Philharmonic Society from 1847. Choral singing especially became established in country town life, encouraged by mechanics' institutes, the Nonconformist churches and the temperance movement, who regarded Handel's *Messiah*, Mendelssohn's *Elijah* and the works of Parry and Stanford as a means of grace for the artisans. Concerts were given by the musical societies in the corn exchanges and assembly rooms. In the summer there might be promenade concerts. Some were held at Banbury's railway station in the 1850s. Charles Sharpe, a seedsman and one of the leading businessmen of Sleaford, opened his gardens in 1859 for promenade concerts of light dance music: polkas, quadrilles and waltzes.

Professional musicians made tours of country towns in much the same way as the strolling players had done. Madame Arabella Goddard gave a piano recital at Sleaford in 1869, performing works by Mozart, Beethoven and Schubert. In its review of the concert, the *Sleaford Gazette* expressed regret that Madame Goddard had not included more 'national' tunes. Perhaps for those the reporter should have attended the concerts of brass and military bands which had wider popular appeal. Regimental bands came to give concerts, but this was also an activity in which people in the town participated, supported again by churches and employers. Town bands were being formed during the 1820s and 1830s, and the larger firms, especially the foundries and engineers, soon had works bands.

Lord Egremont had been among those in the early part of the nineteenth century who were not keen on the strolling players visiting Petworth. Since he had a fair amount of influence in the town there were times when he was able to prevent the companies from appearing there. They were diverted instead to Petworth House, where his lordship and his guests watched a private performance, an arrangement which suited the players since they left richer than they would normally have done. Lord Egremont clearly had no moral objection to the theatre itself, but, he argued, the players' performing in town 'took money out of people's pockets who could not afford it'. The stricter moralists supported such views. The town council at Beccles in the 1860s refused permission for a theatrical company to visit, partly on the grounds that the lower classes' interests would be best served since the theatre 'took away the pence of the poor, which they require for better things.' It was a time when great concern was shown that the minds of the working people should be elevated through such amusements as penny readings and the lectures arranged by the mechanics' institutes.

Even those working men who were happy to elevate their minds were probably none too pleased at being officially deprived of the chance to waste their pennies on the actors, jugglers and other performers. These had always had popular appeal. They were among the major attractions at the fun-fairs. Holloway's Company of Comedians was one of the features at the Nottingham Goose Fair visited by William Howitt, attracting the crowds in usual showman's style with brass band and dancing harlequins outside the tent. The poor were drawn to the players' visits to their towns. They were there peering through the holes in the wall of the barn where John Byng attended a performance at Biggleswade in 1791.

The Vaudeville Electric Theatre at Reading in 1909, offering a
continuous performance of the world's latest productions.

The poor were by no means completely deprived of their entertainment by the strict views of such as Lord Egremont and the Beccles councillors. There were other locations for the performers to go to, which, unlike the town halls, were not controlled by the objectors. Shows such as the 'Grand Moving Panorama Round the World' or the burlesques and minstrel troupes which appeared at assembly rooms and corn exchanges had wide appeal. The price of admission could be as little as sixpence. That may have been a strain on the finances of some working men, but the infrequency of such performances would have encouraged them to find the money.

More cheap amusements were to be found at public houses. These were the homes of traditional singing, dancing and music on fiddle or concertina. Entertainers such as acrobats, singers and comedians gave performances, and from that emerged music-hall. The new theatres built towards the end of the century offered a larger, more respectable home for these variety acts. Star performers such as Vesta Tilley, Dan Leno and Marie Lloyd made occasional appearances, but most artists were less well known and came as part of a touring party arranged through agencies in London. A tour lasting twelve weeks would take the shows to major centres, such as Bristol and South-ampton, and to the bigger country towns like Newark, Bedford and St Albans. Variety was the mainstay of provincial theatres at the end of the nineteenth century, but it did not exclude all other forms. The theatre at Grantham, opened in 1875, emphasised this by changing its name from the Theatre Royal adopted for straight productions to the Empire when variety turns were appearing.

The bioscopes at the fairs were the means of introducing moving pictures to most people during the 1890s. It took a few years before the travelling showmen had any competition in this field, but during the last five or six years before the First World War, cinemas were being opened in the market towns. They were still unevenly distributed. In Wiltshire, no picture palace existed in Salisbury or Westbury in 1915, but nearly all the other towns of the county did have a cinema. In Berkshire, only Hungerford and Wallingford of the county's main towns were without cinemas; Reading had four, Swindon five, but Northampton surpassed both with seven.

From the 1880s the provision of mass entertainment became more important as working people gained leisure time through the institution of bank holidays and Saturday afternoons free from work. Sports, such as football, became spectator events to a greater extent. The privately-owned park at Northampton, Franklin's Gardens, became a less up-market establishment during the 1880s. Special events put on for the Whitsun bank holiday of 1888 included trapeze acts, brass band concerts, hot air balloons, fireworks and illuminations around the lake. Admission for the whole day was sixpence. One of the greatest developments, though, took people away from their country towns for their recreation. The railway companies were quick to offer cheap excursions to all kinds of places and events around the country. Trips to London to see the Great Exhibition of 1851 were among the early excursions, but by the end of the century a cheap day out at the seaside had become a firm favourite.

=7=
To 1914 and Beyond

In outward appearances, the market towns in 1914 were vastly different from what they had been in 1750. Even the smallest had neatly paved streets, lit by gas. They had clean water piped to shops, offices and houses. With new town halls and commercial buildings, shopping streets were more impressive. Some towns had their own buses and trams, a few more their own cinemas. In all these ways and others, the country town had become more urban. The leading industrial cities all had these features whereas even the largest agricultural village was without them.

Although its banks and gas lamps might look the same as those in the industrial town, the activities and attitudes of the market town's inhabitants were often quite different. George Sturt wrote, 'Although Farnham fancied itself a little town, its business was being conducted in the spirit of the village'. He was referring specifically to the fact that in the years immediately before the First World War, his fellow tradesmen at Farnham were still using methods of finance and accounting that would have shocked a Birmingham manufacturer. But Sturt's comment might as easily have been applied to the general character of the market town. Farnham in 1914 was still a modest town of 7,300 people, with hop grounds close by, and a trade that was still of that miscellaneous commercial character that may be described as typical of a market town. Businesses such as the electrical and motor engineers were signs of the times, but the brewery was still one of the main employers of the town.

Not every town would have suited George Sturt's description. There were some, even in the agricultural heartlands of the country, that by 1914 were undeniably urban and industrial in character. The people of Colchester regarded their town as an industrial centre. Rural associations were not always entirely shaken off; Leicester's population of a quarter of a million depended mainly on shoemaking and engineering for a livelihood, yet every market-day the carriers' wagons ambled in by the score bringing villagers from miles around.

The fact that a place like Farnham could be described as being village-like in outlook may be taken as an indication of the relative decline of the market town. Industry had expanded and become more important to the nation, agriculture had become less important and since the 1870s had contracted. Industry had caused the standard of living to rise and had brought new amenities to country towns, but its favours were bestowed unevenly. It was the larger market towns that had the parks, picture palaces, hospitals, libraries and mechanics' institutes. Small towns, which in the eighteenth century had been only one or two steps behind, were now left almost out of sight. Towns like Northleach in Gloucestershire with 900 inhabitants, or Market Bosworth with 650, might have markets and gas lighting in the streets, but they had little else to mark them off from the villages. Trade was entirely rural, with farmers, graziers and market gardeners figuring largely in the directory. Market Bosworth's decline had even gone far enough for one of its societies to call itself the Market Bosworth Village Club.

The First World War brought changes to the routine of market town life, some of which became permanent. The markets held every Thursday at Stow-on-the-Wold were suspended for the duration of the war, but never resumed. Stow lost the high point of its week, the time when it was the focus of the district. Instead, people went to Cheltenham, Banbury or Oxford for their business and shopping. This event perhaps symbolised the new order after the war, but in reality the war was the occasion rather than the cause of the change. The influences on market town life after the war were the same as those before, although some of them had grown more forceful in the meantime.

Agriculture continued to be weak, undermining the rural base of the towns, contributing perhaps to the decline of smaller markets. More important, though, were the telephone and the motor lorry. These carried a step further the process of concentrating markets in larger places. Telephones had been available in some country towns since the 1880s, and motor transport from the turn of the century, but both were in limited use up to 1914. After the war more farmers installed telephones enabling them to do business without attending a market, and when they did go, it was by motor to the major centres. Thus the closure of the market at Stow-on-the-Wold was not too

The market town at war. Military lorries lined up in
Marlborough's High Street in the winter of 1916.

great a loss for farmers of the area, since the big auction marts at
Banbury were within range of their lorries.

The country town's long tradition as an agricultural market centre
may have been entering upon a decline, but as a local shopping centre
it could live on. Motor transport was also opening new possibilities
for future development. One was that new light industries might
come to market towns. In the years immediately before the First
World War, the authorities at a number of small towns had become
concerned about their dependence on agriculture. The councils at
Bourne and Grantham were among those to look into the feasibility
of measures to attract new industry to their towns, but it was not
until the 1920s and 1930s that such policies as building advance
factories were put into effect.

One attraction which a country town could offer to prospective
industrialists was its generally pleasant surroundings, away from the
smoke of the industrial cities. It was an asset in other ways too.
Country towns were attractive places in which to live. By 1914, those
with easy access by train to the cities were already affected by the
movement of richer industrial and commercial families further into
the country. The long lists of private residents in the directories for
Farnham and Hitchin indicate that they were already beginning to be
affected by the outward movement of London's suburbs. The motor

car widened the choice of places in which to live. More people could join those who had gone to Burford for peace and quiet away from the railway lines.

Whether they found the peace they sought may be debatable, for another attraction of the country town was as a place to visit. One of the prominent businesses in tiny Northleach in the 1890s was the Wheatsheaf Family Hotel, advertising its accommodation for tourists. Motor transport helped tourism expand to such an extent that, at times, the people of the more popular market towns must have felt they were being overrun by holidaymakers. But the tourists, together with light industries, the shops and the agricultural services have kept the market town a lively part of the English scene late into the twentieth century.

Bibliography

ALBERT, W. *The Turnpike Road System in England, 1663-1840* (1972)

ALEXANDER, D. *Retailing in England during the Industrial Revolution* (1970)

ALLEN, C.J. *The Great Eastern Railway* (1955)

BAILEY, J. and CULLEY, G. *General View of the Agriculture of Northumberland* (1800)

BAKER, D.A. 'Agricultural Prices Production and Marketing with Special Reference to the Hop Industry in North East Kent 1680-1760' (PhD thesis, University of Kent 1976)

BARNARD, ALFRED *The Noted Breweries of Great Britain and Ireland* (1889-91)

BAYNE, A.D. *Royal Illustrated History of Eastern England* (1873)

BEAVEN, E.S. *Barley* (1947)

BENNETT, JAMES *The History of Tewkesbury* (1830)

BESTALL, J.M. *History of Chesterfield: iii, Early Victorian Chesterfield* (1978)

BINDING, HILARY and STEVENS, DOUGLAS *Minehead, A New History* (1977)

BLAKE, SUSAN 'An Historical Geography of the British Agricultural Engineering Industry 1780-1914 (PhD thesis, University of Cambridge 1974)

BOOKER, JOHN *Essex and the Industrial Revolution* (1974)

BONSER, K.J. *The Drovers* (1970)

BRIGGS, J.J. *History of Melbourne* (1852)

BROWN, A.F.J. *Colchester 1815-1914* (1980)

(ed) *Essex History from Essex Sources 1750-1900* (1952)

BYNG, HON. JOHN *The Torrington Diaries*, ed. C.B. Andrews (1934-8)

CAROE, L. 'Urban Change in East Anglia in the Nineteenth Century' (PhD thesis, University of Cambridge 1966)

CARRICK, T.W. *History of Wigton* (1949)

CARRINGTON, W.T. 'Pastoral Husbandry', *Journal of the Royal Agricultural Society of England*, 2nd. ser. xiv (1878)

CARTWRIGHT, J.J. (ed) *The Travels through England of Dr. Richard Pococke* (Camden Society 1889)

CATHRALL, WILLIAM *History of Oswestry* (1855)

CHALONER, W.H. *The Economic and Social Development of Crewe 1780-1923* (1950)

CHILDS, W.M. *Reading during the Early Part of the Nineteenth Century* (1910)

CLARKE, G.R. *The History of Ipswich* (1830)

COLYER, RICHARD *The Welsh Cattle Drovers* (1976)

COOKE, G.A. *Topographical and Statistical Description of the County of Norfolk* (n.d., c. 1830)

COOPER, ANNA 'Newark in 1830', *Transactions of the Thoroton Society*, lxxiv (1970) pp. 38-44.

'Victorian Newark', *Transactions of the Thoroton Society*, lxxv (1971) pp. 103-14

COPELAND, JOHN *Roads and their Traffic 1750-1850* (1968)

CORLEY, T.A.B. *Quaker Enterprise in Biscuits: Huntley & Palmers of Reading 1822-1972* (1972)

'Simonds' Brewery at Reading 1760-1960', *Berkshire Archaeological Journal*, lxviii (1975-6) pp. 77-88

'The Celebrated Reading Sauce: Charles Cocks & Co. Ltd 1789-1962', *Berkshire Archaeological Journal*, lxx (1979-80) pp. 97-106

CUNNINGHAM, T.M.   'The Growth of Peterborough 1850-1900' (PhD thesis, University of Cambridge 1972)

DAVEY, B.J.   *Ashwell 1830-1914: the Decline of a Village Community* (1982)

DAVIES, C.S. (ed)   *History of Macclesfield* (1961)

DAWSON, W.H.   *History of Skipton* (1882)

DEFOE, DANIEL   *A Tour Through the Whole Island of Great Britain* (1724-6)
The Complete English Tradesman (1727)

DOBLE, E.   'History of the Eastern Counties Railway in Relation to Economic Development' (PhD thesis, University of London 1939)

DUGDALE , J.H.   'Select Farms in the Darlington District', *Journal of the Royal Agricultural Society of England*, 3rd. ser. vi (1895)

ELLIOTT, DOUGLAS   *Buckingham: the Loyal and Ancient Borough* (1975)

ELLIS, C. (ed)   *Mid-Victorian Sleaford 1851-71* (1981)

EVANS, GEORGE EWART   *Where Beards Wag All* (1970)

EVERITT, ALAN   'Town and Country in Victorian Leicestershire: the Role of the Country Carrier', in Alan Everitt (ed) *Perspectives in English Urban History* (1973)

FARRELL, THOMAS   'A Report on the Agriculture of Cumberland, Chiefly with Regard to the Production of Meat', *Journal of the Royal Agricultural Society of England*, 2nd. ser. x (1874)

FIELDHOUSE, R. and JENNINGS, B.   *A History of Richmond and Swaledale* (1978)

FOSTER, ANTHONY M.   *A Brief History of Hitchin Markets and Fairs* (n.d.)

FREEMAN, CHARLES   *Luton and the Hat Industry* (1953)

FYFFE, W.WALLACE   'On the State of our Agricultural Fairs and Markets', *Journal of the Bath and West of England Society*, new ser. xii (1864)

GARNETT, W.J.   'Farming of Lancashire', *Journal of the Royal Agricultural Society of England*, x (1849)

GAUT, R.L.   *A History of Worcestershire Agriculture and Rural Evolution* (1939)

GIBBONS, AGNES and DAVEY, E.C.   *Wantage Past and Present* (1901)

GODBER, JOYCE   *History of Bedfordshire* (1969)

GOODWYN, E.A.   *A Suffolk Town in Mid-Victorian England: Beccles in the 1860s* (n.d.)

GRACE, D.R. and PHILLIPS, D.C.   *Ransomes of Ipswich* (1975)

GREEN, G.H. and GREEN, M.W.   *Loughborough Markets and Fairs* (1964)

HADFIELD, CHARLES   *Canals of the East Midlands* (1966)
Canals of South and South East England (1969)

HERBERT, GEORGE   *Shoemaker's Window* (1948)

HEY, DAVID   *Packmen, Carriers, and Packhorse Roads* (1980)

HILL, MARY   'The Geography of Twenty-five Market Places in Derbyshire and Nottinghamshire from 1861 to 1969' (MA thesis, University of Nottingham 1972)

HOLE, CHRISTINA   *British Folk Customs* (1976)

HOLLAND, H.   *General View of the Agriculture of Cheshire* (1808)

HOME, GORDON   *The Evolution of an English Town* (1905)

HOWELL, DAVID   *Land and People in Nineteenth Century Wales* (1978)

HUPPLE, JAMES, R.   'Abingdon and the GWR', *Journal of Transport History*, new ser. ii (1974) pp. 155-66

JEFFERIES, RICHARD   *Hodge and His Masters* (1880)

JOHNSON, JEAN   *Stow on the Wold* (1980)

KELLY, THOMAS   *Early Public Libraries* (1966)

Life in Old Northampton (anon., 1975)

MACDONALD, S.   'The Diffusion of Knowledge among Northumberland Farmers 1780-1815', *Agricultural History Review*, xxvii (1979)

MARSHALL, J.D.   *Kendall 1661-1801: the Growth of the Modern Town* (1975)

MARSHALL, J.D. and WALTON, J.K.   *The Lake Counties from 1830 to the Mid-*

Bibliography

Twentieth Century (1981)
MARSHALL, WILLIAM   *The Rural Economy of Norfolk* (1787)
   The Rural Economy of the West of England (1796)
MATHIAS, P.   *The Brewing Industry in England 1700-1830* (1959)
MAVOR, W.   *General View of the Agriculture of Berkshire* (1809)
ORR, JOHN   *Agriculture in Oxfordshire* (1916)
PONTING, K.G.   'The West of England Cloth Industry' in J.G. Jenkins (ed) *The Wool Textile Industry in Great Britain* (1972)
POOLE, HELEN and FLECK, ALAN   *Old Hitchin* (1978)
POTTS, W.   *Banbury Through A Hundred Years* (1938)
RAISTRICK, ARTHUR   *Old Yorkshire Dales* (1967)
RANDALL, ARTHUR   *Sixty Years a Fenman* (1966)
REW, R.H.   'English Markets and Fairs', *Journal of the Royal Agricultural Society of England*, 3rd ser. iii (1892)
ROBBINS, MICHAEL   *The Railway Age* (1962)
ROBINSON, DAVID N.   *The Book of Horncastle and Woodhall Spa* (1983)
ROLT, L.T.C.   *Navigable Waterways* (1969)
RUDDOCK, J.G. and PEARSON, R.E.   *The Railway History of Lincoln* (1974)
SANDERS, H.G. and ELY, G.   *Farms of Britain* (1946)
SHEPPARD, FRANCIS   *Brakspear's Brewery Henley on Thames* (1979)
SMITH, B.   'Aspects of the Urban Geography of Worksop and East Retford' (MSc thesis, University of Nottingham 1965)
SMITH, DAVID, *No Rain in Those Clouds* (1943)
SNELL, L.S. (ed)   *Essays Towards a History of Bewdley* (n.d.)
STEDMAN, A.R.   *Marlborough and the upper Kennet Country* (1960)
STRONG, H.W.   *Industries of North Devon* (1899, reprinted 1971)
STURT, GEORGE   *The Wheelwright's Shop* (1923)
   A Small Boy in the Sixties (1977 edn.)
SUMMERS, W.H.   *The Story of Hungerford in Berkshire* (n.d.)
Tales of Old Petworth (anon., 1976)
TAYLOR, AUDREY M.   *Gilletts Bankers at Banbury and Oxford* (1964)
TAYLOR, CHRISTOPHER   *Dorset* (1970)
THOMPSON, PISHEY   *History and Antiquities of Boston* (1856)
THURSTON, H.S.   'The Urban Regions of St Albans', *Transactions of the Institute of British Geographers*, xix (1953) pp. 107-21
TOWNSEND, JAMES   *News of a Country Town* (1914)
TRINDER, BARRY   *Victorian Banbury* (1982)
UNWIN, R.W.   'A Nineteenth Century Estate Sale: Wetherby 1824', *Agricultural History Review*, xxxiii (1975)
VAMPLEW, WRAY   *The Turf* (1976)
Victoria History of the Counties of England (various dates)
WRIGHT, N.R.   *Lincolnshire Towns and Industries 1700-1914* (1982)
WROTTESLEY, A.J.   *The Great Northern Railway* (1979)
YAMEY, BASIL   'The Evolution of Shopping', *Lloyds Bank Review*, xxxi (January 1954) pp. 31-44
YOUNG, ARTHUR   *General View of the Agriculture of Lincolnshire* (1813)
   General View of the Agriculture of Oxfordshire (1813)

Index